"Face facts: What could chard or collard greens or acupuncture do that six rounds of the strongest chemo designed by medical science couldn't do?"

"When you have a life-threatening disease, sooner or later you set the mumbo-jumbo-limbo bar very high. I drew the line only at idol worship, animal sacrifice, or having a substantive conversation with anyone whose title included the word Shaman."

"Prolonged medical treatment with nothing else renders a patient a spiritual wasteland."

"The truth is that 'sweetness' and a good year are for each of us to see and know when we have it. Life is full of ups and downs, some quite consuming and serious. Each of us would be better served to wish that another recognize and count each day and the loving moments it has brought."

"Now I am no longer 'Ned the civil rights lawyer' or 'Ned the Nazi hunter.' I have settled on calling myself: 'The DOJ attorney formerly known as Ned.' I still have a hard time writing 'retired' on all those forms that call for 'Employer.' However, I am still the reigning and champion Funniest Lawyer in Washington. Retirement hasn't changed that."

Facing Up

Facing Up

Grateful Ned's Guide to
Living and Dying with Grace

NED STUTMAN

iUniverse books may be ordered through booksellers or by contacting:

iUniverse
1663 Liberty Drive
Bloomington, IN 47403
www.iuniverse.com
1-800-Authors (1-800-288-4677)

ISBN: 978-1-4401-4099-0 (sc)
ISBN: 978-1-4401-4100-3 (ebk)

Design by AURAS Design, Inc.
Silver Spring, MD

Printed in the United States of America

iUniverse rev. date: 09/11/2009

CONTENTS

NED STUTMAN was diagnosed with mantle cell lymphoma in June 2001. He died on September 17, 2005, five months after his 60th birthday. This is a book he began but could not finish. He left us his words and the task of putting them together. We know he might have done it somewhat differently and we can hear him gently admonishing us for taking advantage of his absence. But, Ned, we're sure you will agree that if many people who knew you, and many who didn't, read this book and learn something about the most important things in life while having some good laughs, then you and we will have succeeded.

Everything that follows, except as noted, is Ned's words. He added the essays and italic interruptions when he began to prepare this book. *Facing Up* is the title he chose because of the double entendre: "facing up" to dealing with his illness and "facing up" to heaven for spiritual comfort.

⌐⌐

Ned and Suzanne

ACKNOWLEDGMENTS

In gratitude to all those who helped edit and design Ned's book

For me, Ned's writings and emails are intensely personal and emotionally thought-provoking. From the very beginning, when he was given his diagnosis of mantle cell lymphoma, he understood that he would have periods of feeling better but the prospect of full recovery was not in the cards for him. Consequently, Ned's thoughts and writings explored the experience of confronting one's own mortality and trying to make meaning of his place in this world. Ned recognized that whatever time he had left on this earth was a gift, and he decided to write about his heightened understanding of what life has to offer. Through five years of illness, he expressed in his writing an appreciation for the ordinary moments of life, immense gratitude for all that he had and recognition of the spiritual and magical importance of love. Understanding the juxtaposition of hope and fear, Ned was able to convey his insights about what really counts with a willing heart, extraordinary integrity, humor, and a searching soul.

I am deeply indebted to many people who helped me gather together all of Ned's emails, photographs, various writings, and letters. The task was overwhelming for me and I sincerely couldn't have done it without the help of so many loving friends, colleagues, and family members.

Sue Singer was there every step of the way. No matter where she was in the world, she read and reread the text, giving suggestions, views, formatting and design ideas, drawing on both her professional expertise as an editor and her personal love for Ned.

Ellen Epstein, the ultimate organizer, systematically collected, labeled, and structured by date each email, read over the drafts and intelligently advised on every aspect of the book.

My children, Shira and Russ, read and reread, wrote and re-wrote their own contributions to the book and gave critical insights. Zak and Gabe gave their important feedback as I sent them different parts of the book.

The design firm AURAS in Silver Spring, Maryland, and in particular Sharri Wolfgang, designed with excellence and creativity and re-organized as needed the writings, emails, and pictures.

My mother, Rose Singer, read the book and cried with profound appreciation and promised me the book would be an enormous success because so many people need to read Ned's exquisite and poignant words.

Jodi Kantor, between her busy life as a *New York Times* reporter following the presidential campaign and a dedicated wife and mother, found time to write the Afterword and give numerous suggestions on publishing.

Congressman Henry Waxman, a dear friend, wrote a foreword without even a suggestion that he might be overwhelmed with work.

To everyone else in my community who encouraged me to put together Ned's writing, I will be forever grateful.

Last but certainly not least, I am grateful to my grandchildren, Caleb, Ma'ayan and Natalia who have given me the joy and spirit to keep going when the project felt too heartbreaking.

This has been a labor of love for me. When we read Ned's words we see how much we can learn from people who face up to their illness and ultimate death and appreciate the potential to live each moment more meaningfully and more completely. Every person in their lifetime should have the opportunity to put together something so meaningful that could potentially have a vital and affirmative influence on others.

Suzanne Stutman

FOREWORD

"When the hour arrived for Rabbi Simhah Bunam of Psysheha
to depart from the world, his wife stood by his bedside and
wept bitterly. He said to her, 'Be silent — why do you cry?
My whole life was only that I might learn how to die.'" *

FATHER GREG BOYLE, a Jesuit priest from East Los Angeles, spends his days counseling and working with gang members. His organization, "Homeboy Industries," has hired hundreds of young men, many of them current or former gang members, and helps bring these men to live what he calls "a dignified life."

In a 2004 NPR interview, he spoke about his experiences as chaplain, surrogate parent, and supervisor to these men. He also spoke about his battle with leukemia, which he was then fighting. "At first, when diagnosed, I was angry," he said (and I paraphrase). "I then realized that I could use this illness as a teaching moment. So many of these men with whom I work at Homeboy Industries are accustomed only to violence and aggression. Through my illness, these men can learn how to take care of someone — can learn how to take care of me. This is my work right now; teaching these men to take care of another human being."

* "The Deaths of the Hasidic Masters" by Samuel Dresner

This is my work right now. In the middle of his illness, in the middle of his uncertainty about the future, he was able to reconstruct and revalue this experience, to sit in it comfortably if not happily, to make it "his work." What a blessing, both for him, and for those with whom he worked.

I THINK A LOT about Father Greg Boyle as I think about my father's five-year-long struggle with cancer. *This is my work right now.* When first diagnosed with mantle cell lymphoma in May of 2001, his "work" (figuratively, if not literally) was similar to that of many upper-middle-class Americans. He worked long hours at his job (prosecuting Nazi war criminals who had subverted U.S. law and made their way to America). He supported and advised his children, helping each of us to navigate our way through relationships and sports teams, college majors and professional careers. His weekends were filled with baseball practice and with spiritual practice, as he faithfully attended synagogue and participated in a bi-weekly Jewish study group. The anchor in the midst of this whirling sea of activity was his adored life partner, my mom.

What was perhaps most normal about this life was that it was, basically and blessedly, an unexamined one. If you had asked my father, pre-diagnosis, what his "work" was (using the term as Father Boyle used it, in a life- rather than employment-related manner), he probably would not have understood the question. None of us would have, really, myself (an aspiring seminary student) included.

And then, as happens so often to become somewhat clichéd, we received the call that made all the difference. His journey, as he evolved from Ned as husband, father, and Justice Department lawyer, to Ned as cancer patient, was one of moving from work to "work," from the unexamined path to the path of reflection and measured days.

READING BACK THROUGH DAD'S LETTERS, one can see the transformation unfold. Initially, when diagnosed, he approached cancer as an enemy in a war. His first letters contain any number of battle- and bout-images. He strongly identified with the Maccabees,* fierce Jewish fighters whom we celebrate on Hanukkah. The battle-imagery was so resonant, both for my father and for the rest of us, that when my son was born, six

---

*A glossary of terms and acronyms begins on page 111.

months after Dad's diagnosis, we gave him the middle name of "Yehudah," after Judah Maccabee, in honor of my father's fight. It was a war, and we were out to win it.

It was the battle imagery with which we were, at first, much more familiar and comfortable. September 11, 2001, the day the Twin Towers fell, was only a few weeks into his first treatment. The timeline of my father's battle was that of America's, as well. But just as America's battles continued to wage longer than expected, so too did Dad's. Ultimately, for him, he realized that what was going to "win" was neither aggression nor complacency, but something in between. Let's call it active acceptance — recognition that the future was decidedly unknowable and somewhat unchangeable, but the present was not. And so Dad began to function in the present. He began to recite, often, his favorite Hebrew prayer, the *Shehechiyanu*, a blessing that gives thanks to the Source of Life for giving us life, sustaining us, and bringing us to this moment. The present was all we had. Every time we would gather in my parents' home, my father would sit at the head of the table, holding court. "This is just perfect," he would say — and mean it. "This is the best day ever." His ability to name and sanctify the mundane, to deeply appreciate the little things — sitting on the porch with a grandchild, or eating good Chinese food — rippled outward. We were all drawn into the "shehechiyanu vortex," the capacity to know and appreciate moments and hours instead of months and years. When it became clear that the quantity of time he had was finite, the quality began to improve.

AS TIME WENT ON, Dad's emails and our conversations began to transform. The battle imagery evolved into something else. And it wasn't that we had given up. It was just that we had chosen a different way to approach the illness. Like a mourner, Dad had moved from anger to acceptance. His understanding of God transformed, too, from being angry and punishing to loving and comforting. In his senior yearbook, my brother Gabriel quotes one of my father's end-of-life quips: "All we got is love, baby."

My father died on the thirteenth of the Hebrew month of Elul, 2005, surrounded by some of those who loved him beyond measure, and whom he loved in return. It was a *mitah yafah*, "a good death," although nowhere near the 80 years plus 3 days that this Talmudic phrase describes.

MY FATHER IS GONE, but his "work" is not. His letters, and indeed the way that he lived his last few years, have left us with a legacy rich with values from which we can frame our own lives, three of which merit highlighting here. The first is gratitude, the sentiment omnipresent throughout my dad's letters. He expresses this gratitude to friends, to family, to those he loves most, and to those he barely knows. A lasting image from his illness is one of hundreds of baseball caps hanging from a chain link fence. When my dad first began chemotherapy, and his hair fell out, friends began to bring him baseball caps by the dozens and even hundreds — hats from obscure teams like the Reading Phillies and hats that proclaimed "Life is Good." During one of his brief bouts of remission, Dad threw a party to thank all of those who had offered support in so many ways. The event was a family walk through the woods, followed by a bagel brunch at a baseball field, the fence of which was adorned by the installation of his extensive hat collection. Each guest received a hat, a brown baseball cap emblazoned proudly with the words, "The Grateful Ned."

The second value I'm struck by in rereading Dad's letters is his appreciation for humanity, his understanding of how important it is to recognize that each of us was created *b'tzlem elokim*, "in the image of God," a basic tenet of Jewish belief. In countless hospital rooms and waiting rooms, Dad made it his practice to treat doctors and nurses, lab techs and custodial workers, each as a unique human being worthy of respect. He knew that this value worked both ways. As he related in an email [page 17] not long after his treatment began, "I now know, from the moment someone enters my room, whether I will be treated like the person I am ... or like McAnderson, 10 Billion Stuck."

Which brings me to Dad's final legacy, humor. Through a sometimes harrowing and often painful journey, laughter smoothed our path. Even on his deathbed, my father was doing stand-up, teasing a single female resident about her dating prospects ("I've got someone for you — email me and I'll see if I can work something out.") or asking an old friend for a kiss goodbye ("at this point, I'm not particularly worried about your germs"). Laughter was a central trope of my father's life. So often now, in his absence, I will find myself in the midst of life's absurdity and imagine his commentary, imagine his ability to burst the bubble of pretension and ground us again in what is most important.

THERE IS NOT A DAY that goes by that I do not think about my father, about the legacy he has left us, about the life that set such a powerful example for all of us and that allowed him, like Rav Bunam before him, to die with satisfaction. When our forefather Jacob was on his deathbed, he, like my father, was able to invoke the blessing of God in his life, "the God who has been my shepherd from my birth to this day" (Genesis 48.15), to bequeath that God to his son, Joseph (48.21). My father raised three children and had a hand in helping raise my husband, as well. We each understand God differently. No matter. What we all share is significant gratitude for the way he lived his life, the way he expressed his understanding of the divine. We all try to emulate it, each in our own way.

I am grateful to my mother, who has spent the last few years lovingly collecting my father's writings for this volume, a tribute to my Dad and to all people who struggle in this world. May we all be blessed to know what our "work" is throughout our lives, and may we engage life with gratitude, humor, and an appreciation for the humanity that we see around us.

Rabbi Shira Stutman

Ned, 1990

APPRECIATION

MY WIFE AND I MET NED and Suzanne Stutman when their family came to Washington, D.C. in the early 1980s. Ned had accepted a job at the Department of Health and Human Services to fight for the rights of the disabled. Professionally and personally he was committed to public service. He had been an attorney in the office of the District Attorney in Philadelphia, when it was headed by Arlen Specter. In the last decade or so of his life, he worked at a special unit of the Justice Department set up to prosecute those in this country who committed crimes against humanity, and especially against Jews, during the Holocaust in Europe.

As a prosecutor of former Nazis and others who worked with them, Ned recognized the need to move quickly before these people, who had so far escaped justice, died off without facing legal consequences for their crimes. Time was running out and the race was on to be sure that justice did not go unfulfilled. We never anticipated that time might also run out for Ned to see this effort through.

Ned was devoted to his family, friends, and community. Despite the demands on him professionally, he took the time to know and be concerned with the lives of so many other individuals. Janet and I became very close to Ned and Suzanne, celebrating many of the Jewish holidays together and seeing our children grow to adulthood.

If it takes a village to raise a child, then Ned was the "Mayor" of our village. At his funeral service, his daughter Shira asked all the young people who felt that Ned had been an important part of their lives to stand and be recognized as "Ned's children." Dozens of young people stood up. They, and my children, in addition to his own Zak, Gabe, Shira, and her husband Russ, were all "Ned's children."

NED EARNED THE TITLE "Funniest Lawyer in Washington" in a competition where he did a stand-up routine. His jokes were never mean or biting. They allowed us to view everyday events and people with a new appreciation and to see the joy and humor in them. If there ever could be humor in chemotherapy, Ned would find it. I called the hospital one day and heard his voice message saying he was "doing great." We knew it wasn't true, but had to chuckle at Ned's encouraging comment.

Ned approached the illness that took his life with courage, spirit, and humor. In these writings, one sees the enormous humanity of a special person who lives on in the hearts and memories of those who knew him. After you get to know him through his words, he will live on through you as well.

Rep. Henry A. Waxman

PROLOGUE

Why This Book?

YES, I AM A CANCER PATIENT, but no, this is not a heart-warming book about having thwarted the dread disease. Nor is it a dramatic but devastating account of succumbing. I have neither survived cancer nor died from it. Thanks to recent advances in medical science, I have been kept alive for four years now, even though attempts to cure my cancer at five major U.S. cancer centers have all failed. While it is not curable, my cancer is deemed "treatable." I have received virtually every treatment that has ever been approved for phase two studies of my particular lymphoma. (Phase two medications are those that have been tested and in use long enough for doctors to have determined non-toxic dosage levels.)

I have a rare, seemingly incurable and particularly nasty form of non-Hodgkin's lymphoma. For reasons I'll explain later, I eschew the word "survivor." I consider myself, instead, a cancer veteran. At a time when more Americans than ever before are living with cancer, I am the future.

I was no sooner diagnosed than I was deluged with cancer-related books from helpful friends — macrobiotic cookbooks and how-to-be-a-survivor manuals, exhortations on becoming a take-charge patient and beating the odds, books on the value of eastern medicine, the importance of specialized nutrition, the virtues of spirituality and homeopathic remedies — enough books to convince me that there was a surfeit of literature on the subject. I was uncertain that I had anything to add.

But now, after being in treatment for four years and seeing the world — the cancer treatment world, at least, in stays at (five star) cancer centers in Baltimore, Houston, Seattle, New York, and Washington — I think, perhaps, I do have something new to contribute. My book inevitably has a kind of Michelin Guide quality.

In his revered psychiatric work *Man's Search For Meaning*, describing his life as a concentration camp inmate, Viktor E. Frankl writes that "[h]umor was another of the soul's weapons in the fight for self preservation." Frankl's work comes closest to capturing the day-to day sense of captivity of a cancer patient. Frankl points out, "humor can afford an aloofness and an ability to rise above any situation, even if only for a few seconds." I have found that humor and irony are ingredients sorely lacking in cancer books, yet laughter is an excellent therapeutic device. What's more, it does not require FDA approval. The ability to recognize and seize upon the incongruities in, and surreal quality of, the cancer world can be every bit as potent a weapon in "fighting the fight" as bravery, vitamin B17, glandular extracts, and a macrobiotic diet.

I was challenged to examine the ironies of living with the disease by the huge outpouring of voluntary help my family and I received from friends and relatives in our community. In my gratitude, I began emailing everyone, reporting on my treatment progress from various cancer centers. Reporting necessitates finding something interesting to say, and for me, humor has always been a favorite source of "interesting." I am, after all, the attorney selected in 1990 as the "Funniest Lawyer in Washington, D.C." Granted, being chosen the funniest of a pathologically unfunny class may not sound like much. Nevertheless the nine minutes of stand-up comedy I had to deliver in order to win the trophy were among the happiest moments of my life.

My emails to friends and family form the backbone of this book. Many led to observations about life and cancer and friendships — about the cancer industry in the United States today, the role of spirituality in healing, the diet dilemma, the way cancer changes you, cancer as a "community disease" and the many ways love, kindness, and the generous support of family and friends can carry a person along this frightening journey.

Facing Up: Grateful Ned's Guide to Living and Dying with Grace combines essays I wrote reflecting on my experience, interspersed with some of my many emails from the cancer treatment trenches of the nation.

I hope this book will have something to say to cancer veterans and their families and friends. But my larger wish is that it be a generic resource for families in all kinds of crises and their friends who ask: "What can I do?" It is a book that would have helped me a great deal had someone given it to me during my treatment.

My Career as an Attorney

I have enjoyed a long and fulfilling career, the bulk of it as a trial lawyer at the U.S. Department of Justice, in litigation involving civil rights, immigration law, criminal law, and human rights.

After graduating from Temple University Law School in 1971, I joined the Public Interest Law Center in Philadelphia, where we worked to get physically handicapped people access to public transportation and developmentally disabled people access to community residences. We also trained the disabled to advocate for themselves using the new laws designed to assure their access to federal programs. In 1979 I moved to the U.S. Office of Civil Rights in the Department of Health, Education, and Welfare, where my work involved developing educational policy relating to handicapped children and adults.

As time passed, I missed the rough and tumble of litigation, so in the late 1980s, I moved to the Special Litigation Section of the Department of Justice's Civil Rights Division, which investigates large scale state-operated institutions on behalf of prisoners, the developmentally disabled, and the mentally ill. Various court opinions had articulated a Constitutional standard for the level of medical and other care to which residents were entitled, and the Special Litigation Section visited and evaluated institutions to see if states were meeting the Constitutional requirements. (Too often they were not, but that's another book.)

My career took a dramatic and unforeseeable turn in 1992, when I was asked to transfer to the Office of Special Investigations (OSI) in the Justice Department's Criminal Division. (This is the unit that tracks down, denaturalizes, and deports, Nazi persecutors who entered the country illegally after World War II.) My work centered on the Nazi destruction of Jews in Poland that began in 1942 and blossomed into "Operation Reinhard," the Nazi plan for their total annihilation.

Denaturalization of a citizen requires a very high burden of proof, almost the "beyond a reasonable doubt" standard applicable to criminal proceedings. This was heavy emotional work. Since much of the evidence involved documentation that was 50 years old, authentication was almost always a hotly contested issue. It was also wrenching to listen to Holocaust survivors relive their wartime experiences in testimony on the witness stand. What is more, virtually all of the defendants had led nondescript law-abiding lives since their immigration and, as the standing joke went, "hadn't gotten so much as a parking ticket." Often their families had no prior knowledge of their wartime exploits. (I often wonder whether my cancer was the result of an immune system weakened by a steady diet of Holocaust horror and sorrow, and the emotion that came from recreating it.)

Utilizing new documentation that had been uncovered after the fall of the Iron Curtain, I litigated 13 denaturalization cases against World War II-era Nazi perpetrators. It was the second day of a trial I had spent years preparing for — the re-prosecution of John Demjanjuk, the retired Ohio autoworker who was stripped of U.S. citizenship because of his service in Nazi prison camps — when my lymphoma was diagnosed. Three years later, on February 8, 2004, I returned to work in the Department. Unable to resume the rigors of my former litigation routine in OSI, I returned to the Civil Rights Division, in the Coordination and Review Section, to focus on ensuring that people with limited English proficiency had meaningful access to federally-assisted medical and educational programs. [On April 1, 2005, Ned retired after 25 years of Federal service, recognizing that his cancer treatments were preventing him from performing up to his standards.]

Discovering My Cancer

For twenty years I ran for exercise. In the winter of 1999, I noticed that I couldn't run as far or as fast as usual. I assumed it was my heart, but a stress test turned out fine, as did a pulmonary function test. I chalked my running difficulties up to encroaching age. I was 55 years old, after all.

After routine blood work in June, 2000, I received a phone call at home from my internist, who had also been my friend for 25 years. In a quivering voice, he told me that my blood test revealed some "anomalies" (a nice word) including an abnormally high protein level. This, I came to learn, signified that a major war was in progress between an as-yet-unidentified invader and my immune system. The search for the invader began. A leading rheumatologist, who couldn't find the cause of the high protein, said it could be nothing, but also suggested oddly that I should "go out and enjoy my life." A hematologist friend told me cryptically that I was the kind of patient that "medical science couldn't help." I didn't ask him what he meant because I was beginning to understand. Something was brewing but it had yet to reveal itself.

My wife stayed convinced it was nothing but bad diet. That is why I love her so.

Throughout 2001, we dutifully monitored my protein level. That May it went through the roof. A CT scan revealed major disease infiltration. In the midst of the Demjanjuk trial in Cleveland, I received the news via telephone from my internist that the disease could either be lymphoma or an industrial strength infection — that is, it could be something, or a much lesser something. My job as a Justice Department Nazi-hunting trial lawyer had taken me to some fairly out-of-the-way places in Eastern Europe. My doctor hoped that I had picked up some weird bug unknown to western medical science.

There was only one way to know for sure whether it was lymphoma or an infection: a biopsy or, as I call it, "cut and paste." The first biopsy revealed no lymphoma but the second revealed "mantle cell lymphoma," so called because of the cell shape. The hematologist who gave me the mantle cell news left me with the impression that my chances for any reasonable survival were slim to none.

For a second opinion, we had the biopsy examined at the National Cancer Institute by the leading pathologist on lymphoma. Her report said "mantle cell lymphoma." Inasmuch as she was the "fat lady" of lymphoma, and she had sung, I had to assume that I had cancer.

Once the diagnosis was made we had to quickly make some decisions about treatment. The M.D. Anderson Cancer Center in Houston, and Memorial Sloan-Kettering Cancer Center in New York viewed me as a solid candidate for any one of a series of lymphoma treatment studies that were being conducted, since I was, ironically, "otherwise in good health." I had three choices: (1) aggressive chemotherapy, (2) chemotherapy, and an autologous transplant (a gathering, and subsequent transplant of my own stem cells back to me), or (3) a stem cell transplant from a donor, if one could be found. M.D. Anderson was running a study of chemo-only treatment and felt strongly that an autologous transplant added nothing. So, on July 27, 2001, to Houston I did go.

I began my first of six-to-eight cycles of "aggressive" chemotherapy on August 8. Most blood cancer chemotherapies consist of toxic cocktails known by acronyms composed of the first letters of the chemicals. My M.D. Anderson regimen had the acronym HYPER-CVAD. Sloan-Kettering favors ICE. Each letter represents a different kind of poison. I felt that chemotherapy for blood cancers was particularly gruesome. Later I would suffer from "chemo envy" when I would meet a person on chemo but who wasn't flattened by it. Each of my cycles was supposed to last 21 days: three to four days of a new "wonder drug" Rituxan, chemo, then about 16 or 17 days for recovery. The toxic effects of chemo are cumulative. The second cycle was harder than the first, but I was buoyed by the prospect of going home and receiving my remaining chemo locally, at Georgetown University Hospital. Before I left, I received my first report card. I got a B minus: I had made much progress but there was something on the scan that my doctors couldn't identify. I flew home on September 18, 2001, seven days after 9/11, on a private jet generously provided by friends. No planes were landing in Washington at the time, and security was tight at Baltimore. My own troubles seemed small in this tragic period.

I had four cycles of HYPER-CVAD at Georgetown, under the supervision of a local hematologist who is a dear friend. Right away, things got tougher. As the effects of the chemo accumulated, I got sicker during treatment, and took longer to rebound between cycles. My cells — white, red, and platelets (blood clotters) didn't return to normal levels. I got pneumonia and lesser infections. I was perpetually anemic. My platelets were particularly problematic and landed me in the hospital with hemorrhage on the horizon. It was 56 days between my fifth and sixth cycles. They tried a platelet-producing drug on me. It put me into cardiac arrest — and no, I didn't see Elvis. But all's well that ends well and, on April 26, 2002, my M.D. Anderson doctors pronounced me "in remission." This lasted until my next CT scan, in November, 2002, when my lymphoma made an encore appearance in my abdomen.

I had to saddle up again. My local hematologist recommended a treatment program in Seattle at the Fred Hutchinson Cancer Center. I actually remembered Fred Hutchinson. In my youth, Hutchinson was the coach of the Cincinnati Reds. I never quite understood how this cancer center came to be named after him, but who cares. I auditioned for the hospital's phase two study sometime in December, and since I was "otherwise in good health" was "accepted" in January 2003. At the Hutch, as it is called, they were doing a chemo-radioactive Rituxan-autologous transplant protocol. I went to Seattle in late January to begin treatment, but I flunked out.

[Ned's last treatment was at Sloan-Kettering in New York City where he underwent a bone marrow transplant on August 13, 2003. Ned lived almost two years longer and died September 17, 2005.]

A TIMELINE

Events on the Tour of the Grateful Ned

WASHINGTON, D.C.

- **WINTER, 1999**
  Ned, age 55, notices that he can't run as far or as fast as usual.

- **JUNE, 2000**
  Blood tests reveal an abnormally high protein level.

CLEVELAND, OHIO

- **MAY, 2001**
  During his participation as lead attorney in the Demjanjuk trial in Cleveland, Ned receives the news that his disease could either be lymphoma or an "industrial strength" infection. Ned returns home immediately.

BALTIMORE, MARYLAND

- **JUNE, 2001**   JOHNS HOPKINS HOSPITAL
  Biopsy reveals mantle cell lymphoma.

HOUSTON, TEXAS

- **JULY 30, 2001**   M.D. ANDERSON CANCER CENTER
  Flies to Texas to begin treatment.

- **AUGUST 8, 2001**   M.D. ANDERSON
  Begins first cycle of chemotherapy.

- **AUGUST 18, 2001**
  Suzanne's and Ned's 33rd anniversary.

- **AUGUST 28, 2001**
  Suzanne's 55th birthday, on the last day of the first chemo cycle.

- **SEPTEMBER 3, 2001**   M.D. ANDERSON
  Receives his first report card. There is something on the scan doctors can't identify.

WASHINGTON, D.C.

■ **SEPTEMBER 20, 2001**
Returns home after 51 days in Houston to continue treatment.

■ **SEPTEMBER 24, 2001**   GEORGETOWN UNIVERSITY MEDICAL CENTER
Third treatment cycle begins as an inpatient at Georgetown.

■ **OCTOBER 19, 2001**   GEORGETOWN
Completes fourth treatment cycle.

HOUSTON, TEXAS

■ **NOVEMBER 4, 2001**   M.D. ANDERSON
Travels to M.D. Anderson to learn whether he needs two or four more
treatment cycles.

■ **NOVEMBER 11, 2001**   M.D. ANDERSON
Verdict: four more treatment cycles needed.

WASHINGTON, D.C.

■ **NOVEMBER 12, 2001**   GEORGETOWN
Treatment resumes in Washington

■ **APRIL 26, 2002**
M.D. Anderson doctors pronounce Ned "in remission."

■ **NOVEMBER, 2002**
CT scan shows lymphoma has returned to Ned's abdomen.

SEATTLE, WASHINGTON

■ **JANUARY 23, 2002**   FRED HUTCHINSON CANCER RESEARCH CENTER
Receives autologous (his own) bone marrow transplant therapy.
Suzanne commutes to Seattle.

■ **FEBRUARY 14, 2003**   HUTCHINSON
Unable to produce enough stem cells, Ned flunks out of the "Hutch"
Autologous Stem Cell Transplant Program.

NEW YORK CITY

■ **MARCH 30, 2003**   MEMORIAL SLOAN-KETTERING CANCER CENTER
Sloan-Kettering doctors fail to harvest enough of Ned's stem cells for an
Autologous Stem Cell Transplant.

■ **MAY 20, 2003**   SLOAN-KETTERING
Ned's New Treatment Plan: a bone marrow transplant from a donor.

WASHINGTON, D.C.

■ **MAY 29, 2003**
Doctors find a compatible bone marrow donor.

NEW YORK CITY

■ **AUGUST 2, 2003**   SLOAN-KETTERING
Enters Sloan-Kettering to prepare for bone marrow transplant.

■ **AUGUST 13, 2003**   SLOAN-KETTERING
Bone marrow transplant followed by reverse isolation. Total time for
Sloan-Kettering transplant and isolation will be approximately 100 days.

WASHINGTON, D.C.

■ **NOVEMBER 1, 2003**
Returns to Washington on the 80th day of the 100-day count.

■ **FEBRUARY 9, 2004**
Almost exactly six months after the bone marrow transplant, Ned
returns to work in the Justice Department, Civil Rights Division.

■ **FEBRUARY 2004 – MARCH 2005**
Nearly always receiving one treatment or the other while settling into a
year of work and family.

■ **APRIL 1, 2005**
Retires from federal service after 25 years.

■ **APRIL 6, 2005**
Ned's 60th birthday party.

NEW YORK CITY

■ **JULY 13, 2005**   SLOAN-KETTERING

Chemotherapy as a prelude to obtaining immune cells from his original donor.

■ **AUGUST, 2005**   SLOAN-KETTERING

Receives immune cells but continues to do poorly. Returns home.

WASHINGTON, D.C.

■ **SEPTEMBER 17, 2005**

Ned dies at Georgetown University Hospital.

Ned and grandson Caleb, 2002

Hats

When Ned first was diagnosed and realized that he would be treated with chemotherapy, he was told he would lose his hair. When people asked "what can I do to help?" he responded they could give him a hat. Hundreds of hats were given to Ned throughout the five years he was in treatment, from all over the world.

All the hats were used in one way or another.

WHO'S WHO

In his letters and commentaries Ned mentions many family and friends.
Here are the connections.

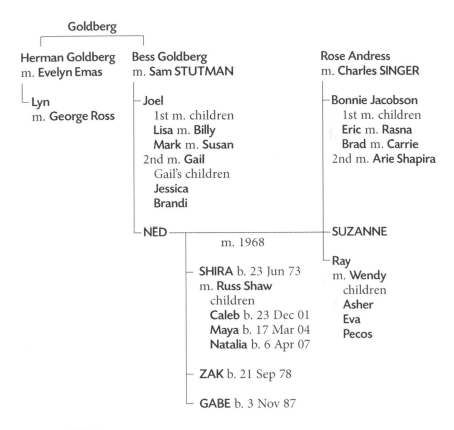

Goldberg

Herman Goldberg
m. **Evelyn Emas**

└ Lyn
   m. **George Ross**

Bess Goldberg
m. **Sam STUTMAN**

├ Joel
│   1st m. children
│   **Lisa** m. **Billy**
│   **Mark** m. **Susan**
│   2nd m. **Gail**
│   Gail's children
│   **Jessica**
│   **Brandi**

└ NED
      m. 1968

├ **SHIRA** b. 23 Jun 73
│   m. **Russ Shaw**
│   children
│   **Caleb** b. 23 Dec 01
│   **Maya** b. 17 Mar 04
│   **Natalia** b. 6 Apr 07

├ **ZAK** b. 21 Sep 78

└ **GABE** b. 3 Nov 87

Rose Andress
m. **Charles SINGER**

├ Bonnie Jacobson
│   1st m. children
│   **Eric** m. **Rasna**
│   **Brad** m. **Carrie**
│   2nd m. **Arie Shapira**

├ SUZANNE

└ Ray
   m. **Wendy**
      children
      Asher
      Eva
      Pecos

FRIENDS

Henry and Janet Waxman

Ellen and David Epstein

Judy and Issie Alter

Lois and George Stark — friends Ned met in Houston

Tom Sacks, M.D. — also referred to as TLS in emails, a long-time friend and Washington oncologist who oversaw Ned's treatment throughout his illness. He was even called in when Ned was dying to help the family with the many difficult issues they were facing.

Jerry Sandler, M.D. — also referred to as JS, a dear friend and hematologist on staff at Georgetown

NED'S LETTERS
FROM THE FRONT

EMAIL IS NOT A CURE FOR CANCER, but it is a meliorator —
a vehicle that forces one to become a storyteller rather than a patient, and
a good storyteller, by definition, must entertain. Thus was born *The Tour
of the Grateful Ned*, the subject heading for hundreds of emails I sent out
to family and friends over the last four years, an exercise that forced me
to find the humor in many a trying situation as part of The Grateful Ned's
Patient Guide to Cancer Centers in Baltimore, Houston, Seattle, New York,
and Washington. It all makes one wonder whether Mr. McGuire's one-word
advice to Benjamin (Dustin Hoffman) in "The Graduate," on the business
with the greatest promise in the future, should have been "Cancer."

WASHINGTON

PREPARING FOR THE FUTURE JOURNEY

July 16, 2001

Dear Friends,

I want to thank all of you for the extraordinary outpouring of support
that has lightened Suzanne's and my load these past two weeks. The
food, cards, emails, notes, voice messages, schlepping, gifts, and internet
research have lifted and kept us upright as we prepare for the future

1

journey. It is a wonderful irony that my life has never been so well organized. I have received warm wishes from close and not so close family and friends, OSI [Office of Special Investigations] colleagues, acquaintances, and people two and three degrees removed from family and friends. People have broken down doors to get me access to medical care. The love and kindness you all have shown to my family simply has been overwhelming. Please forgive me if I cannot thank you individually. You'll never know how necessary all the help has been.

On the medical front, my working diagnosis from GW [George Washington University] pathology — mantle cell lymphoma — has not yet been confirmed by the lymphoma maven, Elaine Jaffee, at NIH [National Institutes of Health] who now has a piece of me. She has a national reputation and it ain't over 'til she sings; we expect that to happen on Wednesday or Thursday. Pending her diagnosis, I am considering being treated at Johns Hopkins Hospital in Baltimore or M.D. Anderson Hospital in Houston where the treatments seem to be producing the best numbers. All that is still up in the air. I love you all, and thank you from the bottom of my heart.
Ned

HOUSTON

FULL OF RESOLVE AND DETERMINATION
July 27, 2001
Dear Family and Friends,
On Monday, Suzanne and I leave for Houston, Texas where I will be examined and likely treated for my lymphoma at the M.D. Anderson Cancer Center (MDA). We leave full of resolve and determination to see this through and come out in remission. If I am treated at MDA, it will be five days on, 14 days off for six serious chemo cycles, after which they will evaluate my situation. ...

[Unfortunately, the remainder of this email is lost.]

This is a message from my 13-year-old son as I departed Washington in July 2001 to embark on treatment in Houston:

Dear Dad,

As you and Mom go off to begin your treatment, I just wanted you to know how much I love and appreciate you and the way you have been tackling "the situation." It is amazing how many people love you and how much they care for your well being. We even had to institute an email network so the phone wouldn't ring off the hook! You touch every person you come across with your gentle, wry humor and your sensitive, loving personality. To complement all that is your strength, both physical and emotional. It is this strength, combined with the love and support of anyone who has ever met you, that comforts me and assures me that you – and we – will come out on top. I love you.

Love, Gabe

HUNKERING DOWN IN HOUSTON

August 1, 2001

Dear Family and Friends,

I am in my second day of testing. I am sitting in the M.D. Anderson Learning Center using one of a bank of computers available for patients and families to send and receive emails, or do research. M.D. Anderson Cancer Center (of the University of Texas), MDACC, employs about 11,000 people. The staff is incredibly well organized and each morning I receive a list of my appointments for that day. The "Office of Patient Advocacy" monitors institutional efficiency vis-à-vis individual patients, and my own advocate appears whenever I have an appointment to make sure that all goes according to the plan. MDACC staff has been completely dedicated to making sure that my experience is the best it can be. And it has been. I spoke with my treating physician yesterday who stated that I was a good candidate for his study which has, to date, put up some good remission numbers. MDACC is truly a multicultural and international place. The one unifying element is cancer — everyone in the building either has it, has a friend or relative who has it, or is involved in treating it. I keep that in mind as I walk the halls or while I am getting examined. It is, in a strange way, comforting since I realize that I am not alone. Here, hardly.

Idle conversation can begin with "what do you have." A parting "good luck" has special meaning. This was the right place for me and my family. Pending further tests, it looks like I will begin treatment on Monday, and have two 20-day cycles here; the next four or six cycles back in D.C. Suzanne and I are planning to hunker down in Houston for 40 days. We have much detail work to do, since Suzanne insists on a place with a kitchen so she can cook for me, although someone gave her the name of a macrobiotic chef who makes and delivers dinners. SWELL!

Suzanne and my brother Joel are stalwarts, and I would be lost without them. Equally, I would be lost without the support you'all have provided to allow us to utilize this option. We are all doing well. Please keep Zak, Gabe, and Shira (baby) and Russ on your radar screens. Love to all, Ned

A THEME PARK FOR CANCER PATIENTS

August 4, 2001

Dear Family and Friends,

It is now Shabbat afternoon, the Sabbath named "comfort," which didn't escape me this day. Suzanne, her brother Ray and I went to Shabbat services this morning at a local synagogue that had a Chavurah-type service as well as the large (really large) sanctuary deal. I met friends of friends and relatives of old Philadelphians. As the gabbai said my name as part of the blessing for sick people, I was reminded of the line from the theme song for the old sitcom "Cheers." Cheers was set in a bar and the theme included the line "you want to be where everybody knows your name." I laughed at the irony as I imagined my name being said in that prayer in many Shabbat services around the nation and realized that it gave me comfort and some cheer.

My brother-in-law Ray and his wife Wendy have been with us for several days. Wendy has been cooking macrobiotically to strengthen me for the road ahead. While it would not be my menu of choice, the food is satisfying and tasty. Wendy is also my T'ai Chi teacher. She is also doing Reiki, which is kind of a healing touch. It's hard for me to accept that the diet and other things are really having an effect but I must admit that they are. In any event, M.D. Anderson offers the same stuff (but not as authentic).

M.D. Anderson is kind of a theme park for cancer patients, offering something for everybody. I am particularly struck by the extent to which the place tries to make the best of a bad situation. Every waiting area has plush comfortable seats and large fish tanks filled with the most beautiful saltwater tropical fish. Naturally, it has a "Wellness Center" which provides nutrition and yoga and meditation and all the services that are now accepted by medical institutions as complementary but a few years ago were regarded as fruity. Incidentally, Suzanne and I no longer refer to me (or any cancer patient) as a cancer patient. We now refer to them all as Maccabees, since they (we) all are fighters in a war.

The Maccabees were a family of Jewish priests that took up arms and led a rebellion against the powerful and seemingly invincible Assyrian-Greek occupiers in Israel. As the history goes, at the successful conclusion of the war, the Maccabees were the beneficiaries of a great miracle from God. Sacramental oil lamps in the Temple burned for eight days when there was only enough oil for one day. Because they were warriors and recipients of a miracle I have chosen the name "Maccabee" as the the nom de guerre for me and all people who have, or have had to battle, cancer.

Suzanne and I have moved to a new home where we will stay for two weeks and possibly more. The home is that of Dr. Hi and his wife. They are on vacation. We have mutual friends and Suzanne has her own history with them. The home is in a lovely section of Houston (near Rice University) and has a pool. They also have a dog and cats. Ray (my brother in law) says it's good to be around pets when you are health-challenged because you get animal energy without eating them.

I think that I will start active treatment on Wednesday. By then they will have finished all the tests. I am anxious to get started.
All my love, Ned

TWO INVADERS FIGHT IT OUT

August 8 , 2001

I began treatment with a wonder drug named Retuxin. You know it is a wonder drug because it has a short name and three pages of possible side effects. I was comforted to know that this anti-cancer antibody has proven very effective in furry lab animals and, with some modifications, in humans with attributes of furry lab animals. It is, in essence, an invader introduced to kill an invader. I now have two invaders in my body and frankly, it's getting crowded. After a brief reaction (chills and fever), I took the whole drip bag that seemed the size of something Juan Valdez would cart around. Suzanne, Zak, and I left MDA at 4:00 a.m. I was glad to get started and pleased about my ability to come back from adversity. Suzanne and Zak were heroic. The number "8" has always been lucky for me, so it did not go unnoticed that I started at 8:00 on the 8th day of the 8th month.

THE PUMP IS NOW MY MISTRESS

August 9, 2001

I reported to MDA at 10:30 for routine blood testing, and went home and slept. I have started a regimen of by-mouth medication used to counteract side effects and side effects of side effects and side effects of the counteracting medication. My brother Joel bought me one of those daily pill sorters that I thought ridiculous when I saw them in a store but now understand their utility. My pill sorter has small slots, which heartens me. Walking out of MDA into the sunlight I passed a Chasidic family on their way in. I wanted to tell them that while the chapel has no Jewish motif or prayer books, there are other places in MDA that do. But I didn't. As I left my eyes fixed on a big no-neck Maccabee (read, patient) with a lineman's physique, the type who would have a number in the 60's, a guard or a center. He was sitting on a bench next to a friend with his chemo dripping from three bags from his chrome schlepper (my name). His gaze landed on me and we nodded. Nods communicate a lot here. MDA patients recognize each other. Through my eyes I wished him all the best and my wish that before long he would be celebrating in the end zone with all the other

Bubbas at Baylor or TCU [Texas Christian University] or Texas. Hook 'em horns. I hoped the same for myself.

Houston is just awful in the summertime. The heat and humidity are heavy and oppressive. Being below sea level, Houston has no underground sewage system, and all raw sewage is carried away in what they call "bayous," which are aqueduct-like open ditches running throughout the city. I immediately got a sinus infection. Houston has been called the most "over-air conditioned" city in America. I can tell you that I was never in a building that was warmer than 65 degrees. I carried a jacket everywhere.

> At 7:00 p.m. I returned to MDA to start my infusion chemo. The drugs used to treat my condition are pretty well known and MDA has no magic potion. They do have a unique delivery system which infuses the medication over 4 or 5 days, 24 hours a day. The Maccabees carry a portable pump around. As I write this, my pump is sitting in my fanny pack on the floor, quietly humming and feeding me a powerful chemo drug. I am content, but know that it's not for nothing that they call my treatment "aggressive chemotherapy" and that much is to come. The nurse gave instructions to me, Suzanne, my brother Joel, and Zak on how to operate the digital pump. Suzanne took notes and, as usual, got the gist. She always does. Joel and Zak argued over what to do when. True Stutmans. It was wonderful. We were home by 9:30 p.m. I slept; next to me my pump and Suzanne, in that order. The pump is now my mistress. Suzanne doesn't mind.

> I have forbidden myself to think the "f" word (fear), but know that after my first course I will lose the apprehensiveness that I get when doing something totally unfamiliar. They tell me I will lose my hair in 14 days. Zak wants to shave my head in a pre-emptive strike. I may let him. The reality has sunk in. Best wishes and love to all, and THANK YOU for the warm notes and cards, books, tapes, hats, amulets of every type. I treat them as reminders of the love from the senders and signs of hope.

> Ned

FREAKING OUT A CLERK IN BANANA REPUBLIC

August 12, 2001

Today was my third day on chemo takeout. Each night I go to MDA and they set me up with two medicines to diffuse in me through a small pump 24 hours a day; one through column A and the other through column B. It has been convenient but carrying the pump/ medicine combo in a mid-size camera bag was awkward. I also learned what it was like to be regarded by the public as a handicapped person, as my camera bag with hanging tubes totally freaked out a clerk at Banana Republic. It was good to shop. Shopping is an optimistic activity, and I feel optimistic. Tonight they changed medicines and I carry only 231 ml. in a small fanny pack with a miniature pump. Light and barely visible. Really great.

Today with Suzanne, Zak, Joel, and my sister-in-law Wendy, I visited the Rothko Chapel. It is a beautiful edifice designed by Mark Rothko in the mid-60's. Rothko also created 14 paintings for it. It is octagonal and neutral gray in color, as are Rothko's large artistic works. Neither the structure nor the art bear any religious markings, and so it is left to the visitor to bring religious or other spirituality to the place. We spent a solemn 45 minutes there, each of us left to our private thoughts. My chemo pump hummed in the background and echoed quietly against the stone walls.

Wendy returned to New Mexico tonight. Her macrobiotic cooking and healing nature helped us all through the early days and gave me strength to deal with medicines. As a parting goodwill gesture, she let me eat bagels this morning. She drew the line at lox.

This morning a nurse asked me about a small red string I wear around my wrist. I explained that this string had rested on the tomb of Rachel in Israel, and was given to me by a friend who believed that it had healing powers. The nurse told me about all the charms, amulets, religious symbols that she has seen, concluding that "you never know what works." I don't rely on magical thinking much, but I do believe that dumb luck, both good and bad, plays a role in our lives. Judaism permits this, as in Mazal Tov. I'm hoping that in addition to the great medical care I am getting, and the prayers and energy from my friends, I get lucky too. That's why I wear a rubber band on my left hand like Wilt Chamberlain did throughout his playing career. I hope to get taller too. As I mentioned before, no conversation with a Maccabee at MDA ever ends without a wish of "good luck." Luck is certainly not good science, but surely as necessary in this endeavor.

Love from Suzanne, Zak, and yours truly, Ned

ONLY AT M.D.A. DO I LOOK NORMAL

August 18, 2001

I finished my first round of chemo on Wednesday night, August 15, and my pump was disconnected. On that night, Suzanne and I slept next to each other without our mechanical domestic partner. (Not that there's anything wrong with that.) It was nice to reach for Suzanne without fear of twisting some plastic tube. But enough about sex. Actually, a little more. Here at MDA they are sensitive enough to advise patients that sexual activity is OK, but may by affected by feelings of anger, fear, and depression caused by the underlying medical problem. Duh!!

Zak and my brother Joel left on Wednesday but a good friend came down to help out for a few days. Zak getting some needed R and R; Joel going to make a living.

Suzanne got certified today to care for my port bandage. It's a big deal. MDA personnel put in a permanent catheter under my collarbone as a port to feed the drugs, and it has to be meticulously cleaned twice a week under sterile conditions. Suzanne took the classes and, even more, toughed out the hands-on competency demonstration. While not squeamish, medical stuff has never been her cup of tea. Kudos.

We have moved to a suite at a local Holiday Inn that has cooking facilities. This arrangement certainly doesn't match having our own home, but we are hoping that it works. Suzanne continues to look for a more ideal place that will carry us for the next 30 days. Our hotel is occupied by what appears to be the entire Saudi royal family who come to Houston for all kinds of medical care — at MDA, Baylor (DeBakey et al). The hotel television system has two Saudi channels, and I caught what I think was the Saudi version of "MacNeill Lehrer." The Saudis obviously favor talking head stuff. Like Israelis, they smoke everywhere.

Tomorrow, August 18, is Suzanne's and my 33rd anniversary. I thought of that today as I looked up from the bed as Suzanne changed my bandage under the watchful eyes of a nurse. Since we promised loyalty to each other "in sickness and in health" 33 years ago, we certainly have had far more "health" than the other and I am grateful. But, for a lingering moment today, I wondered whether this was a little more sickness than we bargained for; 33 years ago we may have been thinking about the flu, or appendicitis. I wished that we were (she was) anywhere else but Houston.

I am in the 14-day cooling off period when my resistance diminishes and I need to take precautions about catching colds or other infections. I wear a mask when I walk through public places. People avoid me. I would too. Only at MDA do I look normal. It is the world of the fifth dimension, with secret codes and acronyms and handshakes and everything.

All the best and much love, Ned

CRAVING MORE INTIMATE CONVERSATION

August 20, 2001

On our anniversary, August 18, after a quick oil change at MDA, Suzanne and I drove to Kemah Beach that sits on Galveston Bay a short distance from Galveston. Speed limits in Texas are set at 70, but people drive 75 (in the slow lane. Welcome Pardner). We made the 45 mile journey in no time. Kemah is a recreational port community, with lots of sail and power boats. It had only a little honky tonk atmosphere. It was more a mix of New Hope, PA, and Annapolis, but with its own multicultural flavor. The temperature was about 98 in the sun, and so we sought the shade of umbrellas at a beautiful dockside restaurant and had a delicious and slow lunch. Kemah is not luscious like Caneel Bay, where we spent our honeymoon, but the boats did remind us of the Caribbean and our first days together as Husband and Wife. It was good to get out. The Docs had told me that while my blood counts were dropping, I should avoid confined spaces with other people, but could spend as much time outdoors as I wanted. So we enjoyed the sun and water and time together. We had a long conversation spanning many subjects long ago put on the back burner. It was a deep, honest, and meaningful conversation, about the past, about now, about our future. It's the kind of conversation you always think you should have but never get around to because of the press of other things. It's the kind of conversation you have when suddenly you have to move everything to the front burner. It was hard and glorious at the same time. It was a thoroughly glorious day.

I lost a few pounds during chemo and not only that, my food intake is now dictated more by cravings and less amenable to carefully planned meals. As a result, Suzanne has relented on her "all or nothing" macro-biotic diet and I have agreed to eat whole grains and leafy vegetables without too much complaint. I have had roasted chicken and baked Salmon (seasoned). We were guests at Shabbat dinner on Friday and I had all the usual (chicken, Kasha, raspberry tort, my favorites). I felt full and happy. The food fight ended in a negotiated settlement.

"Strong opinions" is a minor way of characterizing the food fight presently going on concerning proper nutrition for a cancer patient. The raging battle sometimes has an amusing impact on the cancer patient. The American Cancer Society's dietary suggestions collide head on with Michio Kushi's macrobiotic insistence. A patient willing to try anything will find himself munching foods that are supposed to "kill tumors," while gulping "nutritional energy" drinks, and smearing "macrobiotic sweet vegetable jam" on his toast. Meanwhile, the American Cancer Society wants you to keep the weight on.

I am going to try to call some of you this week. It's good for people to hear me. Hearing my voice will allay fears and concern for my well being. I sound good and, if my sister-in-law Bonnie who just arrived and friend Henry (who just left) are to be believed, I look good as well. As you all know: "It is better to look good than to feel good." My vanity dictates that I mind less being a Maccabee than looking like a cancer patient, and I am determined not to. Not for me, not for my family, not for my friends. But even more, I feel OK. I am still Ned, too. I am still my social self, too, chatting up the other chemo patients in

Longing to Look Normal

THERE ARE PHYSICAL and emotional changes for which you're really sort of unprepared. At the outset of your treatment, whatever it is, you have some sense that you are in for a thoroughly new experience and you know it's not going to be a walk in the park, but you really don't appreciate how it will change you… Forever.

The physical changes are the easiest to describe. And it doesn't make them any easier to experience. You will hear women who have had breast cancer talk about how disfigured they have felt to have a breast removed, or even two, and how it affected their life generally especially their marital life, and how they felt less desirable and less like a woman and all the rest.

The feeling of being undesirable physically and sexually can permeate every interaction. In the hospital I would run into men and women who had had operations on various parts of their bodies, including the head, and you would see the track marks of the scars from wherever, and you realized, number one, that medicine was still at a semi-primitive state where the main vehicle for fighting cancer was to remove it wherever it's found. People who experience that are forever changed, and I don't think any amount of plastic surgery or reconstructive surgery really can deal with that sense of difference you have.

For me, like every other good cancer patient, I lost my hair—not once but several times, depending on what treatment they were giving me. And the chemotherapy drugs are very toxic. They have a lot of other effects on your body as well. You have rashes and your

the clinic. Conversation tends to be a mix of the clinical (How many treatments have you had?) and personal (Where are you from; any children?). Women tend to be more personal and so I like speaking with them more. I now crave more intimate conversation. The "before Ned" and the "now Ned" are not that different. I noticed an adorable U of Houston co-ed leukemia patient that I exchanged a few words with.

eating habits change drastically and your appetite is never the same. And when you are in chemo, you have a kind of chemo-induced ADD which makes it very hard to concentrate and read. People would give me books while I was in the hospital. I could barely read a full article in the *New York Times* newspaper. It also created in me a kind of shortness or abruptness. If I become agitated I can go from zero to 60 very quickly. Because I couldn't concentrate, I couldn't tolerate long drawn out conversations. I needed things to be abbreviated, focused.

It becomes much more primitive. In terms of the physicality, I longed for looking as I used to look. I tended to lose weight when I spent time in the hospital and when people scan you, the one thing they look at is your weight. If you hold your weight, then people think "Oh, he's doing okay." But if you should get thin, then people immediately reckon that you're not doing okay, that you're in a sick state. I really hate the way I look now. I talk to Suzanne all the time. I think of myself as grotesque. I used to weigh 162. I was a vigorous man. Last week when I got out of the hospital I weighed 140 lbs. I'm very conscious of this, especially in relation to my marriage. A man whose whole physical self has changed is going to wonder whether he is still desirable to his wife. I just want to please Suzanne. So when I lose weight, I'm very self-conscious of it and aware of the effect it has on other people. Therefore the most mindful thing I do—I try to keep my weight up. I often say to my wife: I don't mind having cancer, I just don't want to LOOK like I have cancer.

Zak noticed her too. I want to know her story. Everyone here has one. I'll see her again, I'm sure, in one of the ubiquitous quick-stop blood test venues. Most people don't mind start-up conversations. It kills time waiting and most here have an interest in the other. In any other place it would feel like flirting (which, as you know, has never been beyond me), but here not so. It feels more like genuine friendliness.

Today I go for blood testing, a quick shot that stimulates white cell growth and a quick and dirty physical. Easy day. Then, depending on where my blood counts are, Suzanne, Bonnie, and I may walk in the park or maybe drive some golf balls. I am glad Bonnie is here, for Suzanne more than me. They are good sisters to each other.

All my love, Ned Yesterday, Ned Today, Ned Tomorrow
(Motto: Ned to the Third Power)

LOSING MY SIGNATURE EYELASHES
August 28, 2001
It is August 28, Suzanne's 55th birthday, which corresponds to Day 21 on my chemo calendar, which is the last day of the first cycle. As a present, I have presented Suzanne with test results that show all of my white and red cell counts are now back where they should be, prompting my Physician's Assistant to happily exclaim: "You're like a normal person." I told her she was decidedly in the minority if she thought so.

The last several days have been mildly eventful and thus I have been kept from email. I had thought that post-chemo recovery would be a cakewalk but it, too, is an uneven path. I have had some very minor ups and downs but mainly am frustrated that I can't predict anything from day to day. My cousins Lyn and George Ross were with me for six days, and my self-styled hard-boiled New York nephew Billy ("I'm not exactly Mother Teresa") Bondy joined them this weekend. They all get medals for working tirelessly to shape me up to be ready for Round II (Titled: Ned, The War Years). Lyn had to schlep me to the emergency room at MDA on Saturday morning to get some medicine to dull the discomfort created as my bones began to manufacture cells.

She was a real trooper. Didn't avert her eyes once as they poked and injected. At MDA on Sunday, Billy and I spoke Hebrew to an Arab (I think Kuwaiti) in western-style clothing who came four hours too early for his chemo and who didn't have a clue what the nurse was telling him. The man seemed both startled and grateful to finally understand what the problem was, and smiled at me. One small step for man, one giant step for mankind.

George, Lyn, and Billy cooked, cleaned, shopped, schlepped — all making it possible for Suzanne to go home and re-establish family life as we once knew it on Jenifer St. George managed to "liberate" a VCR that we believe was previously resident in one of the Saudi suites. We watched videos of oral histories I took in 1987 (see *Record and Remember*, by Ellen Epstein) of my Mom's extended family (the Goldbergs).

My Mom was one of 10 siblings (13 if you count adopted children). I have about 25-30 first cousins and things increase geometrically from there. Our Seders are Sun Myung Moonian in scope and typically begin with the announcement "Attention K-Mart Shoppers." I was one of the youngest first cousins and always had the best of all possible worlds — the most affection from doting aunts and uncles, and the best of sibling-like relationships with my cousins (with none of the sturm and drang that can go with sibling stuff). It was a near-perfect family childhood. In one way or another, all my cousins have stood up to be counted with me.

Suzanne has returned and brought back the muscle (Zak) for the second round of chemo which begins at 2:00 p.m. on Wednesday. My brother comes on Wednesday. Unlike the first go-round, I take the next dose in the hospital, where I will stay for three or four days. The chemo drug (Methatrexate) is widely used and highly toxic (think "General Sherman's March to the Sea") and so the Docs need to monitor me closely to make sure that they reverse the toxicity at just the right time. This means that like the astronauts going around the moon, I will be out of radio contact with earth for a little while, until I come out the other side. I have a feeling that my first round of chemo was just spring training for this stuff.

Hair: I don't want to dwell on it, but I am now losing it and with it, whatever small differentiation I had from my comrades in the clinic. In some sense, my hair loss represents just a rapid acceleration of a process that began when I was about 32. Rapid thinning is still thinning. I do regret the inevitable loss of my eyelashes. From the time I was five or six years old, my eyelashes were my signature physical feature; they had the power of a quick pick-up line; they spoke volumes. Women loved them. I am only mildly comforted when my nurses tell me that they all will come back. Whatever. I have other fish to fry. By the way, I don't miss the bane of the Jewish male — nose hair.

Thank you all for the books and the books on tape. I have begun to listen to them but expect they will get the most use when I am in the hospital. All the hats are being used. Over the next several days, I will try to respond to the energizing emails I have been receiving. I continue to meet the most wonderful and heroic people. I am humbled by it all. For me, now, courage is just a one foot-in-front-of-the-other thing. I am still watching and learning.

Love, Ned

I REALLY WANTED THE JELL-O

September 3, 2001, Labor Day

Dear Family and Friends,

Houston: The Eagle has landed. I am sitting in my hotel room, having returned several hours ago from four days of inpatient treatment at MDA. As with most things here, MDA makes the best of a situation no one would choose. All rooms are individual, and each is furnished with a Scan-type teak wall unit that hides a Murphy bed (does anyone know who Murphy was?), TV, VCR, and storage. The hospital bed is nifty; it elevates every which way and includes the TV remote so that I always won that battle with Zak. Zak raised the bed about eight feet until my nose almost touched the ceiling, "just to see how high it would go." I hardly minded. Suzanne and Zak stayed a couple of nights; we were like bunkmates and we told ghost stories and it was neat. Then, after they realized that they both needed to sleep in a full bed, Zak went back to the hotel and Suzanne stayed.

Last year, at an increased cost of over one million dollars, MDA instituted on-call room service dining for patients and care givers. Each room has a Marriott style menu and you order what you want, when you want it. It is delivered within 30 minutes by a uniformed waiter (in a tuxedo shirt and vest) who announces, "Room Service." MDA found that there was too much waste, delivering food on a hospital schedule to Maccabees in treatment who weren't ready to eat or who simply couldn't eat what was served. Even the kitchen keeps track of you. One evening when I was feeling queasy, I called for some Jell-O. The young woman on the other end said, "Mr. Stutman, you've requested a pork free diet, and our Jell-O is made from pork enzyme." I told her that the pork free diet request wasn't medical, it was religious and I REALLY WANTED THE JELL-O! I didn't have the energy for a big *Hillel-Shammai* thing, and I'm a Conservative Jew anyway and so I asked her again, this time with more desperation in my voice: "Please can I have the Jell-O?" After which she said (and this is true), "Do you really want to risk it." I laughed out loud, wondering how this young woman knew that the High Holidays were coming. I figured she was right. I don't need any extra baggage this year. We settled on the vanilla pudding.

As for the treatment, as I expected it was stronger and that's why they wanted to watch me more closely. Each time I varied from the path even an iota, there was someone hovering over me, checking my vital signs and doing all the things techies do when they need to know whether I'm getting too much of a good or bad thing. I had a nurse, a pharmacist, a pharmacological nurse, assorted techies, not to mention my Dr. Fellow, and various attending physicians. My intuition has been heightened by my illness: I now know, from the moment someone enters my room, whether I will be treated like the person I am (Ned to the Third), or like McAnderson, 10 Billion Stuck. When I fear the worst, I always make eye contact and ask the techie's name. I tell her (or him) my name, just as a reminder. It's not foolproof, but it works. I always thank the gentle ones. Such positive reinforcement will benefit the next guy. My own doctor, Dr. Jorge Romaguera, saw me this morning and actually released me. He has such a soft manner. He has such soft hands. Like wide receivers and infielders, doctors need soft hands.

I wish I could tell you that I went through this round with the bravado of John Wayne in "Sands of Iwo Jima," but it simply wouldn't be true. The drugs were stronger, I had more of everything and there was once or twice that Suzanne, Zak, and my brother, had to jack me up and get me going. From time to time Mr. Nice Ned disappeared and was replaced by Mr. 'Zilla Ned. Although I attribute the change to having been transformed through the miracles of modern chemistry into Mr. Love Canal Ned for a few days, Suzanne would have none of it and put a stop to it. She kept me up and running. One afternoon, Suzanne literally held me up and carried me (and my rolling chemo-stand) around the pod while I was completely zoned out on anti-nausea medication. Suzanne, Zak, and Joel all earned their large salaries this go-round.

My chemo cycle ends on September 18, the first day of Rosh Hashanah. Roughly about that time I will be undergoing a series of tests to find out how successful the treatment has been. It is ironic that my fate for the coming year will be recorded in a series of high-tech scans and other tests at the very same time that, according to medieval High Holiday Jewish imagery, God will be inscribing my fate for the coming year next to my name in the Book of Life. I am hopeful that this coincidence is auspicious, and that God will find enough credit in me to give Him justification (with or without a little spin) to give my many friends and family who worry about me and me a healthier year. Surely God knows what I have discovered by accident — that cancer is a powerful catalyst for change. I think more powerful than 1000 *Ahl Cheyts*. I have changed in many ways already, and have made a great many promises to myself about how I will be in the coming years. I hope that God knows all this and doesn't mind the hint.

I received a lot of emails while I was in the hospital. Zak read them to me and they were great. I will try to respond to them in the next several days but may not be able to get to them all. Please don't interpret this as a hint not to email. I love receiving them.
Love, Ned

Cancer as a Community Disease

WHAT I LEARNED, and what my family learned, is what it takes to stand up against a terrible illness. To quote a phrase— "it takes a village" to stand up to something like this. I often would feel sorry for people who are in it alone. I remember being in Houston, going for an x-ray, and I was sitting in the waiting room with half a dozen people. It's always freezing cold in all these places because the machinery has to be kept at a certain temperature level. An older African American man comes in and sits next to me. The nurse comes in and brings me a blanket, and this guy is sitting there in a kind of flimsy shirt, and so I got a blanket for him. The nurse said "Are you with anybody?" and he said "No." And I thought to myself how could anybody go through this alone? I always felt sorry for people who were alone.

As a matter of fact, it's very odd to see someone in a cancer hospital alone. Usually patients come with an entourage. Hospital entourages at any cancer clinic anywhere would always be the same. You'd have the cancer patient and if the patient were someone my age it would be his wife with him, and she would have the notebook to take the notes, plus have all of his records, and if it was an older person, it would be his children, and they would carry the notebooks and the records and they would listen and say "Dad do this. Dad go here." It's really very stylized. In the entourages there are note takers and there are schleppers. An entourage is necessary because as a patient, when the doctor starts talking and you have something like cancer, listening systems shut down. There was only so much I could absorb, and so I needed another pair of ears there because after a while, I would say yes to anything! Suzanne was doing this for a long time for me. I think it speaks to what is essential to combat a serious illness. You just can't do it alone, and your family can't do it alone, and you just have to have a network.

*This prayer was written in response to the previous email, by friend
Ellen Epstein:*

RE: SEPTEMBER 3, LABOR DAY

September 3, 2001 11:35:54 PM

Dear G-d:

I am forwarding the email of Ned Stutman to you to make sure you put
it on the top of your pile of "Must Reads." I know you are omnipotent
and omniscient, but I just wanted to make sure you didn't miss this one.
Ned has an incredible cadre of family and friends who want to make
sure he gets inscribed in the Book of Life, not just for this year but for
many, many years to come. I am not sure how one goes about asking
for an inscription (doing a *mitzvot*? davening daily? being a good Jew?).
But whatever your criteria may be, I want to assure you that Ned and
all of us who know and love him can testify to the fact that he deserves
to be inscribed. See what you can do. We all have complete and utter
faith that you can do this.

I feel confident that without asking their individual approval, I can sign
the name of all of us around the world who are on Ned's email list that
they, too, join me in this request.

With complete and utter sincerity,
Ellen Epstein

SUSTAINED BY MY CONNECTIONS

September 9, 2001

Dear Family and Friends,

This has been a good week. I have been visited by Issie and Judy Alter
and Ellen Epstein. Judy is a gourmet cook and came at just the right
time as my appetite returned. Issie is a physician (OB/GYN) and, among
other things, accompanied me to Anderson and walked through all my
appointments. Delivering babies is much nicer, but he never let on. Judy
and Issie brought a video of portions of their recent Bar Mitzvah
celebration, and so I saw many of my family and friends. I saw Shira in
her maternity clothes (for the first time) leading an egalitarian Shabbat

dinner. I knew it was egalitarian because Shira asked both men and women to light candles. (Only the women really knew the drill.) Ellen came as the Alters left, thereby allowing Suzanne to go to Santa Fe for our niece's Bat Mitzvah. Ellen has been taking care of me for a couple of days now and is especially good at recognizing potential problems and doing advance planning. Issie, Judy, and Ellen all cooked, shopped, cleaned up, and brought great cheer. In addition, Ellen incessantly corrected my grammar. Ellen wants to be the first Grammarian General appointed to the cabinet, and I think she'll make a good one.

On Friday night, new friends, Houstonians Lois and George Stark, came to the hotel for Shabbat dinner. Lois brought a catered dinner for about ten people (I am still eating it). The Starks lost their 21-year-old son Daniel after he waged his own battle at Anderson. Lois now serves on the pain management committee at Anderson, which the facility named after her son. She has graciously become my guide and advisor on a great many things, starting with navigating the waters at Anderson and onward and upward from there. Lois has been especially insightful about my experience. I feel like I have known her for years. As a final endorsement, she looks like she belongs in my extended family. When she and my cousin Lyn were in the same room together, they looked as if they could be sisters.

Today is Day 12 of my treatment cycle and all my cell counts are bottoming out as I write; the last treatment was really powerful. But, other than being a little more tired than usual (from low red cell counts), I don't feel much in the way of changes from the change in counts. Nevertheless, this is a time when I am on guard against infection and monitored by Anderson in case I need a boost of one thing or another. This being the weekend, I have not had to have my counts taken. It is welcome to have a couple of days where my visits to Anderson are brief in-and-outs (vital signs and a shot). Tomorrow they will take my counts and I will know more. I am doing well.

One thing I have learned from this experience is how well connected I am. I don't mean politically or financially. I mean that I have become aware that over the years I have made connections with people that have endured time and distance, not to mention disagreements, insults, or misunderstandings. I have received the most beautiful and heartfelt notes and emails, not only from my contemporary family and friends, but also from long-not-seen members of my extended family, old, old friends, and former colleagues. All have brightened my days and lifted my mood when that "count" has been low. I hope I never forget how I was sustained by my connections. I also hope that everyone has some connections to draw on if they are ever needed. At the end of the day, they are all that matter.

Love to all, Ned

9/11 SUFFOCATED ANY CREATIVE IMPULSE

September 23, 2001

Dear Family and Friends,

I am home, having arrived on Thursday, September 20, and am happily occupied surveying the landscape of needed minor household repairs (in my absence we are down from four to one working toilet) and bills that are long overdue. Shabbat with my family (including my mother-in-law, Rose Singer) was especially sweet. As for Gabe, it is as if we never left. It was nice to have the weekend off while I felt so good. I felt the baby move in Shira's belly. It was worth the wait.

I have not written for a while because the events of September 11 completely suffocated any creative impulse as well as rendered my own situation far less consequential, even to me. Like everyone else, I have been a jumble of deeply felt emotions that were dictated by the calamitous events of that day. My own personal ups and downs hardly mattered. I hope that none of you have lost a loved one or friend in the disastrous attacks.

FYI, before I left Houston on Thursday, my doctor gave me an excellent report card. I think that God laid a heavy hand on the latest diagnostic test results since they disclosed that I had made complete progress in several areas and major progress in one. I continue treatment tomorrow, Monday, September 24, at Georgetown University Hospital. Georgetown has virtually no capability for ambulatory treatment (i.e., chemo takeout) and so I will be spending a lot of my treatment time as an inpatient there. I probably will want some company. Don't be surprised if you get a call. I think most Rabbis would agree that idle gossip is permitted in hospital rooms if the purpose is to lift the spirits of the patient.

I hope you all know that Suzanne and I could not have survived the 51 days in Houston without the family and community support we received at home and in Texas. Rosh Hashanah was the loneliest day for both of us. My counts were low so we couldn't take advantage of any of the several dinner and luncheon invitations we received from an extraordinarily generous Houston community. Nor could we implement our plan to steal a few moments at the Rothko Chapel. Instead, we stayed in the hotel and I quietly recited the Torah portion that I have read at synagogue for the last 15 years. I did this at roughly the same time Gabe was pinch-hitting for me this year at synagogue. It is my secret that each year, before I read Torah, I exploit my vantage point on the Bimah (stage) by quietly surveying the 1600 people who have gathered together to worship in the Kay auditorium. I especially cast my gaze on my family and friends and satisfy myself that everyone is in his or her proper place and the picture is right and complete for the beginning of the next New Year. I never imagined that it would be me who would be missing from the picture, but no one ever does. That thought, I suppose, is one of the central themes of the High Holidays. It is my determined hope that I will be back in my regular seat next year with my family and friends nearby. This and all the rest that goes with it would not be possible without the endless love and help Suzanne and I received from my family and friends.
Ned

Cancer Is a Powerful Catalyst for Change

CONNECTIONS AND MORTALITY. Everybody experiences their sense of mortality differently. In my case the kind of cancer I have, the kind of lymphoma I have, they say is not curable, but it is treatable. I've received virtually every treatment that has ever been approved for phase two studies — phase two meaning that they know what the dosage should be and they know the danger levels for the stuff that they're giving me, as opposed to phase one, where they're testing all this stuff out.

I've always had a sense that I knew where it would end, despite the confidence and the optimism of all my doctors and my family. I always was a realist in the sense that this was a disease that hadn't been beaten yet — that they were doing a lot of research and I would be lucky if it happened to me, but I held out no real hopes that it would.

So in a sense, believing I knew where it would end, I had a different mindset. In the beginning, I was preparing for the end. One advantage of having a long-term illness is that you have an opportunity to prepare and put your affairs in order. And by affairs, it means a lot of things. Not only personal affairs, your will, etc., it means preparing relationships. It means addressing long held trivial grievances that needed to be addressed. So it's given me some time to just… Repair.

If I had an acquaintance but we had drifted apart for some real or imagined slight, I made an effort to reconnect. And I did that with several people with whom in the course of things I'd become disconnected, either because of some competitive sense either of us had regarding our children, or something like that. In the ordinary course of life these things happen.

I didn't want to leave relationships unfinished. Realizing two important things made a difference for me. One is I had the opportunity over the course of my illness to experience a great outpouring of affection from the people in my community. They supported me and my family and are continuing to do so. I can't begin to list the many ways we were supported. And some of the people I had either forgotten or lost interest in were front and center in this battle, and it was a good reminder about what our relationship had been. I've read about people who write that some of their friends didn't show up for them. I have not experienced that, except for a single person. Everybody showed up for me. And so when I was able, I wanted to follow up and get back into a social or personal connection with them. I found everybody was responsive.

Second, I discovered from this experience how well liked I am. It reminded me of an experience I had when I was about 36. I was living in Washington at the time. My high school reunion was in Philadelphia and I didn't really want to go. As has been the case in my entire marriage, Suzanne forced me to go. She said "Go, you'll have a good time." My high school years were very difficult times. I went to a very competitive high school and my memories were fraught with the unbearable intellectual wake of those years. Those were not the years when parents knew how to resource their children. My parents just didn't pay attention to me. It wasn't as though they realized "he's having a problem with math" and got me 18 math tutors!

When I got to the reunion a little late, all my high school — it was all boys — were waiting to be seated for lunch, and they all rushed me. And it reminded me of how well liked I was. It's almost as if I needed a reminder. Now and then this illness reminds me of that. As I grew up I never thought of myself as a truly lovable person, so all of this led me on a mission to use the time I had to repair relationships.

There was more complicated repair needed. There were people I still didn't like. I was going to try to make an effort to fashion whatever connection I could and try not to hold a grudge. To appreciate them for themselves and not demand that they be more like me or less like who they were. Family members fit into this category. You have certain members of your extended family that you see often but you may not like. I decided to make an effort to get over that hurdle because those grievances have a way of spreading outward and influencing others. If you don't care much for somebody, those feelings become known.

I realize it's not possible to love everybody. But what I said to myself — and I'm not saying I've been totally successful at this — but what I said to myself was "When I leave I don't want to leave with anyone feeling that I was purposely unkind to them." *I have moved into forgiveness.*

WASHINGTON

BATTING CAGE WITH GABE AND CHINESE DINNER

September 28, 2001

Dear Family and Friends,

It is 7:30 a.m.. on Friday, day five of my third treatment cycle. A nurse just took my vital signs (as seen from a medical perspective) and they are good. Yesterday was Yom Kippur and I spent it quietly with Zak and my prayer book. I read the prayer book with the kind of care that solitude allows, took responsibility for those sins that were mine (more than I would have liked), but felt mostly gratitude. Cancer is one of those really big things that easily drive out all good news and it was easy to forget how much our family had to be grateful for this year. Zak graduated from college with honors and GOT A PAYING JOB; Shira was awarded the prestigious Wexner fellowship and is in her first year of Rabbinical college; my jewel son-in-law Russ got the job he always wanted (Headmaster of the Abington Friends Middle School); Shira and Russ bought a new house in East Germantown (Philly); they are going to have a baby in December; my beloved mother-in-law is with us in good health; Suzanne is her usual terrific self. I felt a lot of gratitude.

After a lovely weekend "off" with high blood counts and normal activities (Family Shabbat dinner; batting cage with Gabe; big Chinese dinner) I entered Lombardi Cancer Center of Georgetown University Hospital on Monday to continue my treatment. Although initially I was disappointed that Georgetown required that I do this round of treatment exclusively as an inpatient (whereas at Anderson I took the chemo as an outpatient), I have now gotten with the program here and have forgotten about it. Mostly I have tried to appreciate that M.D. Anderson was the first and only treatment center that I knew and that any change would be difficult. At Georgetown, for the most part I have had senior charge nurses monitoring my Anderson treatment protocol under the watchful eyes of Tom Sacks, my hematologist/ oncologist, and Jerry Sandler, a dear friend and hematologist who is on staff at Georgetown and daily hovers around the floor to make sure that staff is mindful of me. The director of Lombardi Cancer Center came for a visit the other day and, although Georgetown is a new and unfamiliar treatment setting for me, I am beginning to feel comfortable with my situation here. To ensure the most intense nursing coverage, Tom has secured me a room on a hyper-hygienic floor that houses hematologic patients, including many immunologically compromised bone-marrow transplant candidates. I know many of you would love to visit but the hospital has rules about numbers and kinds of visitors on this air-locked floor. In any event, I have settled in and daily realize (with deep gratitude and satisfaction) that I am home.

My family life is regaining some semblance of normalcy. I read the *Washington Post* in the morning and watch and complain about dreadful local news which I missed desperately. Suzanne can sleep at home, work, take care of Gabe, and swing by as needed or desired. Zak can do the same. Shira and Russ get down on weekends. I have had some visitors and feel generally, that I am where I need to be now. I miss work but more, I miss my friends from work who have carried my load without complaint and only good wishes for me. Happily, I am no longer anyone's full-time job. I have a lovely window in my room through which I can watch energetic Georgetown students (read "leer at Georgetown co-eds") going to and from classes. (One day after Yom Kippur and already I am guilty of "wanton looks." Go figure!) My outlook is bright. If all goes as planned, I will complete this round of treatment on Sunday and get to one of Gabe's baseball games in the afternoon. But as in all things, time will tell. Biggest surprise of this treatment cycle thus far: yesterday they told me that my chemo created a kind of temporary diabetes so I had to give up a heavenly blueberry cake for six hours. Life could be worse.
Love to you all, Ned

PUTTERING DURING CHEMO OFF-SEASON

October 27, 2001

Dear Friends and Family,
It's been a while since my last email. The world news has been so incessantly dreadful that it has been hard to work up a head of creative

steam. But my lack of motivation has been completely trumped by my gratitude for the wonderful meals that have been prepared by many of you. Chicken recipes of every imaginable kind, roast turkey, *challahs*, soups, great vegetable dishes, and assorted other foods — all have made our lives here immeasurably easier and better. Naturally, all this largesse has given rise to a budding commercial venture and I will soon publish a cookbook featuring all the wonderful recipes. I have no working title. Suzanne has already rejected *Feed Your Head*.

It is now Day 13 of my fourth treatment cycle of 21 days. I finished this, the "B" and more toxic cycle, at Georgetown on Friday, October 19. I am between treatments — what I call the chemo off-season (or Hol Hamoed Chemo) — and I spend my days puttering around the house and trying to maintain otherwise good health, despite having very little in the way of an internal health maintenance system. So far so good. I travel to Anderson on November 4 for three days of testing to find out how I am doing and whether I will have to undergo only two more treatments (and finish by December 24) or four more. I am hoping and praying for only two. I miss you all and long for the day when I am in more normal circumstances and can be with you all again.
Love, Ned

FALL MIDTERMS AT M.D. ANDERSON – STILL STUFF LEFT

November 11, 2001

Dear Family and Friends,
Last week I had my fall midterms at M.D. Anderson. I brought to them all the confidence of a student who had done all his homework, attended every class, and read all the required texts (not Cliff Notes). The good news is that I am making steady progress. The bad news is that I am making steady progress, but there is some stuff left. We all had hoped that I would be in remission by now. The bottom line is that I will now have four more treatments (instead of two). This means that I will not finish treatment until roughly mid-March (my calculation). My doctor is confident that I will be in remission after two more treatments. Suzanne and I were disappointed at the news but are readying ourselves for the road ahead. If I didn't before, I now know to

a certainty that treatment is far from an exact science. We'll see what the future holds.

Inasmuch as my blood counts were normal during the test period, the last week has seen a return to normalcy for me. I have visited with friends, actually eaten in restaurants, got the car washed, thrown the ball with my psycho-dog, and have not wigged out every time someone sneezes in my presence. Although the news from the front could have been better, all in all it has been a great week. People who see me tell me I "look great" but I secretly ask myself "compared to what." When I look in the mirror, I don't see myself anymore. I don't look terrible (Could Ned really ever look terrible?), even for a guy who has had four serious bouts of treatment. But I do look less like me than I did before. Losing my hair (everywhere) makes me look like one of those weird Egyptian hairless cats, or a naked adolescent action figure (Ken). (I now cherish my long lost eyelashes more than ever.) Also, my pretreatment body reflected the 13 or so years of running and conditioning weightlifting that I had done to give myself a chest and shoulders (which I never had as a youth). All that is gone now. Randomly redistributed. Looking at the temporary changes the treatment has made in me, as much as I am able I am more keenly empathic with women who are forced to sacrifice breasts in the first assault on their disease. In this war, such women are like the Special Forces.

I start treatment at Georgetown tomorrow, November 12. It is the "A" round which I have tolerated fairly well. Your generosity seems endless. It is endlessly appreciated.

Talk to ya', and Love to all, Ned

This is an excerpt from a note from my son-in-law:

November 17, 2001

"Perhaps a person gains by accumulating obstacles. The more obstacles set up to prevent happiness from appearing, the greater the shock when it does appear, just as the rebound of a spring will be all the more powerful the greater the pressure that has been exerted to compress it.

Care must be taken, however, to select large obstacles, for only those of sufficient scope and scale have the capacity to lift us out of context and force life to appear in an entirely new and unexpected light.

"For example, should you litter the floor and tabletops of your room with small objects, they constitute little more than a nuisance, an inconvenient clutter that frustrates you and leaves you irritable ... cursing, you step around the objects, pick them up, knock them aside. Should you, on the other hand, encounter in your room a 9000 pound granite boulder, the surprise it evokes, the extreme steps that must be taken to deal with it, compel you to see with new eyes ... Difficulties illuminate existence." – Tom Robbins, *Even Cowgirls Get the Blues*

Dear Ned,

Here's to your 9000 pound granite boulder, and the getting around it, over it, past it. I love you, I support you, I believe in you. You help me to see the world differently. I will help you deal with this boulder however I can (Caleb will too).

Much love to you, Russ

RIDING IN AN AMBULANCE WITH SIRENS BLARING

December 16, 2001

Dear Family and Friends,

We are awaiting the birth of our first grandchild. Shira's due date is tomorrow, Monday, December 17th, but we all expect her to be a little late since Suzanne was late with Shira. Shira and Russ are completely ready for prime time and so are we. Although it's risky to predict such things, it looks as though I will be a fully eligible participant in post-delivery events, including the bris. This is because I was unable to start my sixth round of chemo on the target December 3rd, because one of my counts (platelets) was, and remains, too low. I apologize for inconveniencing any of you who adjusted your schedule to sit with me during the aborted treatment. My doctors tell me that my bone marrow is slow starting up, having been battered by my five prior industrial-strength chemo treatments. I have been very frustrated waiting around two weeks for my stubborn bone marrow to start up,

Better to Look Good Than Feel Good

FINDING PLEASURE IN THE MOMENT and finding displeasure in the mirror — these are some of the changes cancer brings into your life. Large goals are replaced by small ones — usually a passionate desire to return to the same old, same old, the way of life you took for granted before you got cancer. In the world of the cancer patient — and, judging by fashion magazines on the market today, only in the world of the cancer patient — you can be too thin. Even though weight loss is usually a result of the chemotherapy that is attacking your cancer — and not the cancer attacking you — the public rarely processes this. Weight loss earns you many a sorrowful look from friends, a kind of involuntary squint in the eyes that lets you know you look pathetic. For social purposes, it's better to look good than feel good. Right now I am 20 pounds below my fighting weight and dress up to look good. Still, I get sorrowful glances from my family and friends. Can't be helped.

but I have also benefited from the delay. My immune (white) cells are decent so I got to watch Gabe play in two basketball games for Smith Jewish Day. Gabe scored nine and eleven respectively, with a bucket of rebounds and several nice, thread-the-needle assists. But the real beauty of his game is in all the things he does that don't show up on the score sheet — how he moves on the court. I am close to my old self because after the game, with his typical equanimity, Gabe asked me not to shout instructions to him in the middle of play.

My own life hasn't been entirely dull either. On December 14th my doctor gave me a shot of a relatively new drug that is designed to increase platelet production and I had an "event" that landed me on the floor in my doctor's waiting room, then in an ambulance and into the emergency room and cardiac unit at George Washington University Hospital (for about 24 hours of observation). While I was

Gabe, proud Dad Russ, Zak holding his nephew Caleb, and new Mom Shira

out (briefly), I don't think I went over to the other side because I saw neither white light nor Elvis. Nothing looked like heaven to me, either. Anyway, it was neat riding in an ambulance with the sirens blaring. My courtesy bus driver that day, Ellen Epstein, got more than she bargained for as she watched me come out on a gurney feet first from my doctor's building and sat with me in the emergency room (getting me checked in) and sitting with me until Suzanne got there. Never a dull moment. Bottom Line: I am home, and fine and dandy.

It is the seventh day of Chanukah, the Jewish holiday commemorating a miracle. The daily, endless, kindness of our family and friends reminds me that there are miracles still. I don't know how you all continue to do it. I'll let you know when my situation changes and I can start up again. Love to you all and a joyous and happy new year to all of us,
Ned

WORKING IN CHEMO BETWEEN HEALING AND ACUPUNCTURE

January 27, 2002
Friends,
It's been some time since I have written, but my life has been in reruns. For those of you who missed the last several episodes: *When we left*

our handsome male lead Ned, he was supposed to begin chemo on December 3. But blonde buxom Biloxi-born Nurse Kimberly burst into his room, naked, and drawled: "You can't begin chemo today. Your blood count is too low. You might get really SICK" [emphasis added]. They made love. And so it went until January 24 when blonde buxom Biloxi-born Nurse Kimberly burst into Ned's room, naked, and declared: "I do declare! Your counts are up and you can begin chemo again." They made love. In the midst of this, during the week of January 14, in the custody of his indefatigable cousin Lyn, Ned traveled to Houston where former Enron executives now employed at M.D. Anderson Cancer Center performed all manner of tests on him and pronounced him "Good." These results were certified by accountants from Arthur Anderson. They all made love.

Fade to commercial.

I probably will begin chemo again in the next week or so, if I can work it in between my healing and acupuncture sessions. Because my body was in open rebellion against the treatment for six weeks, the doctors are reducing my dosage, turning the toaster down to dark brown instead of burnt. It's a shame I have to start again because my hair has been growing back. I have to shave and my short head hair gives me a sort of rugged Sigourney Weaver "Aliens III" or Rutger Hauer "Blade Runner" (The Director's Cut) look. I dread losing my hair again.

My new grandson Caleb flourishes, even while his parents walk around in a sleep-deprivation-induced stupor. Caleb has a sweet smile, a lovely disposition, and the deep visual concentration of his parents that suggests he inherited their great intellect. That's great, but I bought him a pair of Air Jordans to ensure his proper development.

I credit all of you for my recent good test results. All the prayers, thoughts, good wishes, cards, photos, books, and other material and psychological support have made the difference for me, Suzanne, and my family. Out of respect for my loving wife, I am also crediting her leafy vegetables (spinach and kale). There will be more to this tale. I will keep you informed.

Love to all, Ned

P.S. Go Eagles!

LOCATING FREE RANGE ORGANIC KOSHER CHICKENS

February 12, 2002

Dear Friends and Family,

First, some really good news. Responding to Suzanne's call, diligent friends have located a butcher (in New York) that sells free range

---

Others' Reactions to Serious Illness

MY YOUNG SON, Gabriel, when asked how he's doing with all this, says that to his mind it's all the same. I get up, I go to work, I come home. He says when something changes he'll react. That's what he says. When he can perceive a real difference, he'll react. Gabe is 17 and he is looking at colleges. He's going to be a high school senior next year. We filled out a parental form that questioned "Is there anything unique about your family life that would shed light on your child?" So I wrote a paragraph describing how so far for four years of Gabe's high school life, he's had to deal with this situation and he has nonetheless achieved wonderfully. He's shown great courage. He's really been amazing. He's done well in school. He's done well socially.

My 26-year-old son, Zak, has been more involved with me clinically. He's actually taken me to the emergency room and sat with me for 5-6 hours and he's stayed with me in the hospital room for a couple of days so he's been more involved with me in a clinical aspect. He's more connected emotionally with me and this disease.

I think that the family crisis has brought the two boys together in a very, very complete way, helped by the fact that my older boy is living at home. Often we sit at the dining room table the four of us, talking for hours. We miss our daughter Shira and son-in-law Russ, but they are in Philly. They have two kids.

I GET WEARY responding to the public all the time. People will ask me how I'm doing. I've tried a million responses to the question of how am I doing. I decided to say I'm fine. I'm doing just fine. And then I thought well, that's not completely accurate so maybe you should be more honest. And I started to say something…

organic Kosher chicken. Since they were free range, I'm sure all the chickens were much happier before they were, well, you know. This is a good find because I fear Suzanne was prepared to order from London or cart 200 or more live chickens from Frederick, Maryland to a kosher butcher in Silver Spring in the Saab. On another front, my

"I'm hanging in." And then I'd say "Well, compared to what? Compared to some things I'm doing great, compared to other things I'm not doing so well." So basically I decided it was a throw away question, so I'd just say "I'm fine" instead of giving one of the eight different levels of answer.

Suzanne always says I'm fine. No matter what. I could be in the hospital for two weeks; she'll tell everyone "He's fine. He's doing great."

I NOW ALWAYS STOP when I see a homeless person who asks for a donation — if you can call it that — I now stop and talk to them. From time to time in the past I'd give a homeless person some money, but I never stopped to talk to them. But I decided a while ago that I was going to see what kind of response I would get. So now I stop after I give some money and ask him how he's doing. I get a lot of shock and surprise from these homeless people — shock that anybody would want to talk to them. As a matter of fact, there was one guy whose attitude was that he was working and didn't want a conversation. You know how when you barge into the office of your supervisor and you want to have a conversation and he responds non-verbally that he doesn't really have time to talk. I got the sense from one guy that I was in his office — which was this corner — and he wanted me to make a contribution, but he didn't want to have idle conversation when there was someone else coming down the street. So they're businessmen in many respects. But I just thought it was like treating them less as an object than as a person. Goes hand in hand with the concept of appreciating the moment and wanting to be treated as a regular guy, not with pity but with respect.

grandson Caleb is growing and giving pleasure to us all. He visited this weekend and Suzanne (and Shira and Russ) took him to one of Gabe's basketball games. Nothing lights up Suzanne as does her grandson and she and other Moms and Dads sat in the stands playing with this wonderful baby. My limbo may end soon — maybe Thursday. All my counts are good and have been for a couple of weeks now. One more test on Wednesday to make sure. Then another round of treatment beginning Thursday. We'll see.

Love to all, Ned.

OVERCOMING FEAR OF HUGS AND KISSES

April 7, 2002

Dear Family and Friends,

I can't remember the last time I wrote. So much has happened. After a longish delay, I had my sixth chemo treatment and — a two-week bout of pneumonia aside — have recovered from the chemo quite nicely. My counts bounced back much quicker than expected and my weight too. Like the cherry blossoms on the Tidal Basin in Washington, my hair is also starting to bloom. I went to two wonderful Seders, one with my extended family (of about 94) and the other with my immediate family. I have eaten my first fresh salad in eight months and no longer scrub my grapefruits with anti-microbial soap before I cut them. I celebrated my 57th birthday yesterday and now know to an absolute certainty that birthdays are good.

I start back at the Department of Justice tomorrow, albeit on a limited schedule. I visited my office on Thursday and was met with an outpouring of welcome from my colleagues that touched me deeply. All in all, my life is slowly moving to a kind of normalcy, although I am surprised that re-entry too, has its challenges. I have to overcome eight months of fearing hugs, friendly kisses, and groups of more than four. My sneeze and cough sonar has to be squelched considerably. I also realize that I must now turn attention outward and take care of those closest to me who have taken such good care of me while I have been unable to do so. Although I was not AWOL from their lives, there is much catch-up work I have to do now for, and with, my family. Although my Washington doctor has told me I am in remission, the Texas doctor has yet to use the "R" word. But even he, too, in recent conversation has made rumblings that I may not need further treatment. I will visit Texas next week for another round of tests and his final opinion. I hope it is *"no mas."*

All in all, I feel as though my life offers the possibility of bloom again. So, you can all feel free to delete my name from any list of persons in need of healing blessings. I know that there are people who need them more than I do. And even though I hate to give this up, since I am cooking and shopping now, you are all off the hook for that too. If we need something, I will call.

I visited with a dear friend last week who asked me how I got through the treatment period. I was surprised how I fumbled the answer. As I thought more on it, I realized that I didn't walk through those months as much as I was carried by my Suzanne, my loving immediate and extended family, my dear friends and colleagues, and by what felt like the immediate world. Although I have tried to thank people for individual gifts and acts of kindness, I have been too absorbed for thank you notes and the like. I am ashamed of that failure. Just know that for the last 10 months I have felt, as one friend put it, as though you have huddled around me and my family in the world's largest embrace.

Thank you and love, Ned

NEVER IN MY WILDEST DREAMS DID I EVER IMAGINE THAT THIS TREASURE COULD BE DEPLETED

June 28, 2002

Dear Friends,

The time has come when I am forced to ask for leave donations.

As most of you know, for the better part of a year I have been in treatment for non-Hodgkin's lymphoma. "Lymphoma" is a cancer of the lymph system. While there is no cure for my cancer, there are treatments that have added years to a patient's life. I am grateful that my chemotherapy regimen, begun last August at the M.D. Anderson Cancer Center in Houston, Texas, and continued at Georgetown Hospital, has gotten me into remission. The effectiveness of my treatment was magnified by the kindness and generosity of my family and friends, including many of you, who helped me immeasurably during this time. I now have hair on my head, and am back at work in the Office of Special Investigation about 60-75% of the time, depending. I am working out a little at the gym and taking long walks to get back into some reasonable shape. I feel better than OK most of the time and blessed all of the time.

When I was diagnosed in late May 2001, I had accumulated about 110 hours of sick leave and several hundred hours of annual leave over my 22 years of government service. Never in my wildest dreams did I ever imagine that this treasure could be depleted. Well, as the man said, life is what happens to you when you are planning other things. My leave will be exhausted this pay period. The leave bank has extended me some leave but I will need far more to make up for my reduced work schedule, periodic appointments with doctors both here and in Texas and, given the relentless nature of my particular cancer, likely further treatment in the, hopefully, more- rather than less-distant future. Since I have been accepted into the leave bank program, I am no longer allowed to accrue leave even though I am working 60-75% of the time.

All of this forces me to ask you, sooner rather than later, to donate annual leave to me through the Leave Transfer Program. I am keenly aware that donation of annual leave represents dollars out of your pocket. Any DOJ employee inclined to contribute should ask their timekeeper for the Authorization to Transfer Leave Form. Other Federal employees should ask for Request to Donate Annual Leave to Leave Recipient (Outside Agency) (Optional Form 630-8). FYI, my full name is Edward Allen Stutman; Department of Justice, Criminal Division, Office of Special Investigations. I am sorry that you must endure bureaucratic red tape for your act of generosity but this is, after all, the government.

To rejoice in the day, and in gratitude for all you have done to help the Stutman family this year, Ned, Suzanne and family invite you to a Rock Creek Park fun-run, bike, hike or t'ai chi form (you choose), followed by refreshments, on Sunday, October 6, 2002.

Athletic activity begins at 9:00 a.m.; light fare to follow at approximately 10:00 a.m..

Location: Candy Cane City athletic complex on Beach Drive off East-West Highway in Chevy Chase, Maryland. We have reserved the Candy Cane field house just in case of rain and hope to get a field early in the morning at the intersection of Beach Drive and Pinehurst Parkway. Look for the Big Banner identifying the site. Kids welcome.

Please RSVP by September 25

I had hoped I would never have to write this email. At the same time, I am thankful to be here to do it and to have friends and colleagues to whom I feel comfortable sending it. I thank you for any generosity you are able to show and regret that I may never be able to fully repay it. Thanks for reading.

Ned Stutman

PS: You may forward this to anybody who knows me or who you believe might otherwise have a specific reason to contribute leave.

SEATTLE

CAN ANYONE SPARE FREQUENT FLYER MILES?

January 15, 2003

Dear Friends,

On January 23 I will be going back into treatment for my lymphoma which has recurred. But the good news is that I am going to Seattle, the epicenter of good coffee, grunge rock, and great Pan-Asian food. I will be treated at the Fred Hutchinson Cancer Center, or the "Hutch" as it is called in the ever-expanding cancer biz. The Hutch is small by Houston's M.D. Anderson standards, but it too has broken ground for a huge building. The Hutch is affiliated with the un-small University of Washington. I will be receiving a chemo/radioactive retuxin/autologous (my own) bone marrow transplant therapy. I'll be radioactive for 10 days and in immuno-impaired recovery for about 10 weeks. It was the radioactive part of the treatment that really sold me. Instead of the ordinary menace I have been, I always aspired to become a radioactive mutant menace like in all those '50's movies — "Them" (giant ants in LA), gonzilla (lizard in Tokyo), or "The Attack of the 50 Foot Woman" (that's some woman). Watch for my story at your local theaters: "The Dreadful Ned Devours Puget Sound." Artistic integrity requires that it be filmed in Japanese with English dubbing. A deeply felt "thank you" to all who were tested and/or volunteered their bone marrow but I have chosen to use my own. I would have been honored to be your blood brother. Don't be offended. It's not about you; it's about me.

Our plan is for Suzanne to commute to Seattle each Thursday morning and return to Washington on the Sunday night red-eye to work and parent Gabe for part of the week. Shira is to come down from Philly to take care of Gabe for the remainder of the week and otherwise, we have put Gabe up for adoption on e-Bay and have received generous offers from some wonderful families who promise to raise him as the little Buddha he is. Zak likely will be on full time duty with me in Seattle, beginning in mid-February. I have a short list of people — mostly family and (active) retirees — who have volunteered to come to Seattle for a week and who I think can do it without undue personal or financial hardship. Don't feel obligated to volunteer. It's a major, major, major, deal.

Seattle is quite beautiful, especially when "the mountain (Rainier) is out" as the locals say. In the beginning, Suzanne and the family will be staying at the Residence Inn by Marriott on Lake Union. It's lovely but we may move into Hutch housing as it becomes available. We'll see.

Because Suzanne intends to commute, and Seattle is not Baltimore, we would greatly appreciate any frequent flyer miles any of you could spare. If you have close family or close friends in the Seattle area who you think we would like to know, please connect us. Suzanne and Gabe would greatly appreciate any meals you are inspired to cook. Suzanne loves cooked greens. Gabe loves, well, basically flesh and potatoes and anything except milk products. Shira will be there too and she is pretty much a vegetarian. Caleb eats whatever. We will try to develop some organization to all this.

All in all, things are under control. I'll try to stay in touch.
All the best, Ned

Ned and
Suzanne
in Seattle

DO'S AND DON'TS IN SEATTLE

January 25, 2003

Dear Friends and Family,

I am avoiding large crowds in anticipation of treatment. I am sending a photo of Suzanne and me taken on Thursday, January 23rd at Lake Union which is where our hotel is located. As you can see, I buzzed my hair a little to avoid hair on pillow which inevitably follows chemo. The temperature was a balmy 46 degrees and a little overcast but the sun was out most of the day. The beauty of this place assaults you and creates a wonderfully relaxed feeling. Every waiting room at the Hutch faces the lake. Great planning. The Residence Inn is delightful. All in all, the accommodations couldn't be better. Last night Suzanne and I went to the home of a dear friend of a dear friend for Shabbat dinner. It was wonderfully warm. We dined with two couples and two of the people were affiliated with the University of Washington (U-Dubya, don't you love it). They couldn't have been lovelier. As an aside, sentiment for the war out here is lukewarm, to say the least.

Based on my limited observation of the locals, I offer the following: "Do's and Don'ts in Seattle":

- Don't wear LL Bean.
- Do wear Northface.
- Don't refer to your possessions as "things" or "stuff;" every inanimate object here is "gear."
- Do carry an umbrella but never use it; it marks you as a visitor.

■ Do use your windshield wipers; but always keep them on the lowest interval, no matter if you are in a monsoon.

Clinical Notes: I had some tests and met with my doctor, Ajay Gopal. He was born in India but raised in Atlanta. My counts were OK (for me) except my bothersome platelets were a little low (For JR's, GS's, and TLS's benefit they were 63, but who's counting). If all is in order, I will start my chemo on Monday or Tuesday. End of Clinical Notes.

On his eight-tape set ($121.00), rivaling in length Winston Churchill's biography, Deepak Chopra [M.D.] tells me that I should not accept the notion of mere coincidence; and that there is a certain synchronicity in life which, while not scientifically measurable, can be meaningful. And so, these are some of the meaningful coincidences that have occurred: (1) When I alighted the plane on Wednesday, the rain stopped and the sun came out; (2) I have met several people in this town who know several people I know thus reaffirming what I have always suspected — most everyone in the U.S. is just two or three degrees of separation from the Grateful Ned; (3) In Seattle for a bone marrow transplant is Dani Shotel, the young special ed teacher from the Washington D.C. area, to whose bone marrow drive many people contributed for her (and me). Suzanne met her mother in the exercise room at the hotel and it turns out that I went to college with her father who is a professor at GW. (I think I knew that.) In any event, synchronicities abound. Deepak would smile.

Ellen Epstein has been informing us of the incredibly generous outpouring of Frequent Flyer miles. Managing all the numbers will no doubt qualify Ellen to be a Hedge Fund manager. FF miles make a big difference in our ability to play this hand. Thank you to all who are feeding our growing boys. Gabe and Zak are loving the meals.
Love to all, Ned

SALMON IS THE "CHICKEN OF THE NORTHWEST"

January 30, 2003
Dear Friends and Family,
Shira is here in town and, between treatments we visited the U of Washington mall. Although the university is quite impressive, the mall

"I am the third fish from the bottom on the right."

is Montgomery Mall generic, with Anthropologie-Gap-Sunglass Hut-Office Depot-Eddie Bauer and on and on. Houston has the same thing at Rice University. U-Dub does have a lot of local specialty shops with local artist jewelry that is quite creative and distinctive. I don't know about you but I make it a practice never to shop in any store that is piping Eagles music, especially "Hotel California."

As you can see from the picture, I have started treatment. I am the third fish from the bottom on the right. In case you didn't know, salmon is the "chicken of the Northwest." There is steelhead, king, and endless other varieties. There are pool-raised and ocean-caught (free range, so to speak). You should always purchase the ocean-caught. They have more nutrients. Many of you know that I have had my problems with salmon in the past, but I am trying to get over them. Frankly, I have little choice. They know little of chicken out here. It's salmon, salmon, salmon.

HARVESTING AND HICKMAN

February 7, 2003

Dear Family and Friends,

Well, if all goes according to plan, on Saturday or Sunday the doctors will be "harvesting" my stem cells. In this context, the use of the word "harvest" seems odd. It conjures up little combines plowing through my blood collecting, baling, and loading my stems cells on flatbed trucks while doctors in John Deere hats sing "Oklahoma." Actually, they use a machine that filters stem cells from my blood and returns the blood to me. Stem cells are immature blood cells. If my stem cells are anything like me, they're extremely immature. The doctors have spent the last ten days getting me ready for this procedure and tonight, February 6, they begin the final countdown. I'll know tomorrow if the numbers are right. The chemo I received on January 28 was more powerful than I thought, and I was neutropenic for about four days this week. Neutropenic doesn't mean "without a penic." It means that my white blood count had zeroed out. Now the count is back on the rise. My bout was a reminder that the path is never smooth. I had brazenly forgotten that.

Tomorrow they put in my cathether or "central line," named "Hickman" after the doctor who invented it. It so happens that Dr. Hickman is affiliated with the Hutch and he actually still puts catheters in one day per week. When I heard this, being such a star-worshipper, I began insisting to anyone who would listen that Dr. Hickman put mine in and sign it. It would be like having a catch with Cal Ripkin. But the timing couldn't be worked out. I am still going after a picture with him. His card must read: "Eight million inserted."

My cousin Lyn Ross and her husband George were with me this week. Naturally, I gave them more than they bargained for, but nothing fazes

Cousin Lyn Ross with husband George, Ned and Suzanne

them. Suzanne arrived today. The Seattle community keeps our hotel refrigerator full, and the Washington community does the same at home. Shira and Caleb are in Washington to look after Gabe together with Zak. Things are good. I am trying to keep focused.

Most people are not called upon to exhibit courage on a systematic basis for a prolonged period of time. Cancer requires it in large doses. It is the mother of all frightening events. People with cancer need courage-boosts at regular intervals. Unfortunately, unlike adrenaline, courage isn't something the body automatically manufactures on an as-needed basis. You have to get it from other places. Sometimes the absence of choice is the foundation for courage.

TREATMENT STALLS – STEM CELLS NOT COOPERATING

February 11, 2003

Dear Family and Friends,

This is a self portrait taken in our new apartment at the Pete Gross House. Pete Gross was a sportscaster for the Seattle Seahawks who had to receive cancer treatment around the country and was struck by the lack of support for traveling families. This apartment house was established in his memory. We have a nice view of the Space Needle and other local sights, including the so-called rock and roll museum

Self portrait
with Space
Needle

built by Microsoft demi-mogul Paul Allen. The architecture of that building is its only saving grace.

The sun has been out every day. Everything is perfect about the situation except that my body is not cooperating. I have not yet mobilized enough stem cells for collection. I have been in this waiting place before but still find myself getting frustrated. The Doc has not given up, but the next week or so will tell the tale. The other day, as my treatment stalled I spent some quality time in the small Hutch chapel sorting things out. I took a blessing from the "blessing bowl" and it read "May you Find Peace Today." I'm the kind of man who saves things like that, and fortunes from fortune cookies too. It became clear to me that if this treatment plan was meant to be it would happen. If it wasn't, it wouldn't and I would have to shift to Plan B. You know you have a good spiritual moment if you feel better going than coming, and I did.

The kindness of the local community is overwhelming and sustaining. Meals magically appear. People call and visit. People make themselves available for me if the need arises, day or night. People pick up Suzanne at the airport and take her back. Suzanne tells me that it is much the same at home. Thank you to everyone. Zak comes tomorrow and I am excited to have him.
Love to all, Ned

FLUNKING THE HUTCH TRANSPLANT PROGRAM

February 14, 2003

This is Zak and me at a local park on the Sound [following page]. Zak is consoling me because I just flunked out of the Hutch Autologous Stem Cell Transplant Program. I was not able to produce enough stem cells. The Doc said the only way to get me more stem cells was to give me growth hormone. He told me that this had been tried on a limited basis in Milan, Italy. The 13 Italian subjects all produced more stem cells but it is possible that I could end up looking like Andre the Giant, except with bigger feet. I don't think so, but I haven't ruled it out completely. I have always been dissatisfied with my feet.

Ned and Zak at Puget Sound

Anyway, as you know, this is the second treatment program I have flunked and so by now, I think that my photo must be on the hematologists' web site with the notation "DON'T TREAT THIS MAN." There are only so many studies I can skew before someone takes notice. In the future, I intend to apply for treatment under an assumed name. I am now looking squarely at Plan B which is a mini-matched unrelated donor (MUD) transplant. In this procedure, I receive marrow from a matched donor but the treatment leaves some of my own marrow active and unaffected. This option has always been there, both at M.D. Anderson and at Seattle as well, but I chose to try the high-dose radio-immunotherapy first. Some of my most astute advisors secretly wanted option B in the first place. Now they may get their way. I don't know where I will have this procedure done, but Seattle seems to be winning hands down among my family and friends. It's such a lovely environment. I am, nevertheless, going to check out the procedure at MDA and Johns Hopkins Hospital , too. In the meantime, as we set the wheels in motion for this, we are coming home, probably in the next few days. Thank you from the bottom of my heart for all you did to make this attempt possible. It simply wasn't meant to be. Love, Ned

NEW YORK

LIFE CAN BE FUN EVEN JUST GOING AROUND IN CIRCLES

March 23, 2003

Dear Friends and Family,

A quick note to let you know that the Grateful Ned's next tour stop is New York at the Memorial Sloan-Kettering hospital (don't forget the hyphen) on March 24. As you may recall, my last stop was Seattle where my body didn't cooperate and failed to produce the stem cells necessary to complete treatment. Well, the doctors at S-K think that they CAN harvest stem cells and have started prepping me. We'll see. If I can make it there I can make it anywhere. The doctors say they need six million stem cells. The irony of the number was overwhelming. In any event, we'll know by Wednesday whether the Bowery's up and the Battery's down or something like that.

Otherwise, all is well. I have learned that life can be fun even though you are just going around in circles.

Love, Ned

Going around in circles with grandson Caleb

Dog walkers on Park Ave.

STEM CELL WELL RUNS DRY

March 30, 2003

Dear Family and Friends,

My treatment in New York is going a little slower than expected and I am interviewing for part-time work. Above is a picture of my first group interview. A typical Park Avenue crowd. I bow-wowed everyone but the Bijon (on the right) who thought I was just a little too unsophisticated.

Sloan-Kettering harvested stem cells from me on Monday, Tuesday, and Wednesday of last week, but by Thursday the well had run dry. My body's stubbornness continues to amaze the medical profession. All told, I delivered a decent number — 1,700,000. My doctor originally told me that he needed 6,000,000, but being New York, I assumed that was the retail price. We hondled and he now tells me he will accept 2,300,000. Nobody pays retail in New York; why should I? My doctor gave me a two week vacation after which he is going to try to harvest me again.

While in New York I spent several days living on the Upper East Side in my wonderful sister-in-law Bonnie's apartment. Her building has a DOORMAN. Living on the Upper East Side, I immediately had the urge to purchase a house in the Hamptons, a large SUV, and enroll Gabe in Riverdale High School. For the time being, I resisted all of these. I visited the Guggenheim and spent quality time with my son Zak, too. That part was heaven. I went out to dinner with Bonnie and her husband Aryeh. Aryeh graciously picked up the check; first time in 17 years. I must be sicker than I think.

Love to all, Ned

WASHINGTON

COMPATIBLE BONE MARROW DONOR FOUND

May 29, 2003

Sparing no expense and searching far and wide, my doctors have found what they refer to as a "compatible" marrow donor for me. We were obviously separated at birth.

Ned's marrow donor?

I know that I have not written for a while, not wanting to compete with other popular reality programing such as "American Idol" and "Joe Millionaire." But the long and the short of it is that "Ned's Excellent Adventure, Depending" continues. I am pleased to report that if all goes as planned, in the next month or so I will be heading to Sloan-Kettering Hospital in New York to prep for a bone marrow transplant that will follow. A donor has been found, although further fine-tune compatibility testing remains and he (I presume) must also undergo a physical exam and "harvesting." If things go well, though, I will be in New York for a total of 20 weeks, although I will be incommunicado for much of that time — especially in the beginning. If things don't go well, let's just say I'll be in New York for a shorter time. Of course you probably have guessed that the above picture is just my idealization; the search procedure doesn't allow a recipient to know the donor's identity for at least a year, and thereafter only at the donor's discretion. Although in many ways I am unique to a fault, hematologically I am rather ordinary which turned out to be something of a good thing. Notwithstanding this match, and leaving no stone unturned, my S-K doctors have asked that my children, niece and nephew, and multitudinous cousins be tested for compatibility. I have promised full reading-immunity at the next Passover Seder — especially the paragraph with all the Rabbi names (i.e. Tarfun, Azaria, etc.) — to any relative who submits to testing. Although I appreciated the personnel and care I received at the Hutch in Seattle and adored the many friends Suzanne and I made there, I have decided to have my transplant at Sloan-Kettering because: (1) it is closer to home; and (2) S-K has more and better cable channels.

I don't know exactly when all this will begin, but probably before late-June. The start depends on this and that. The plan is for Suzanne to commute to N.Y., and stay from Thursday through Sunday with her sister Bonnie and my brother-in-law Aryeh while I am in the hospital. After I am released, Suzanne and I will be staying together elsewhere at a place to be identified. Suggestions welcomed. Gabe will have a July full of baseball and hanging out at Cosi in Bethesda. He will be watched over by my 34-year-old nephew Eric Jacobson (Ph.D.) who shortly will be arriving from England where he heads the Jewish Studies Program at Sussex University. Eric will be staying in our home during the summer while studying as one of the first group of Kluge Scholars at the Library of Congress. Anyone who can, please keep Gabe (and Eric) on their radar screen.

This is sort of an anticipatory, hopeful, and catch-up email all in one. As in all human events, each planning day brings much joy and some challenge. We'll see.

Love, Ned

P.S. My grandson Caleb can dunk on his three-foot basket.

IN GOOD HEALTH EXCEPT, OF COURSE, FOR MY CANCER

July 1, 2003

Today I began my three-day regimen of chemo at Georgetown as a prelude to another three-day regimen in mid-July as a prelude to my bone marrow transplant which is to occur at Sloan-Kettering sometime in early August. I say all of this with the certainty of a man who knows there is no certainty; that any plan is only a plan, and that every bump in the road means more time in the repair shop. But, overall, I am trying to be ready for all of this, with the emphasis on trying. The really good news is that my doctors are happy that I begin this experience in good health except, of course, for my cancer.

My 34-year-old nephew Eric Jacobson is with us for this go-round. He has been in Europe for the last 10 years or so, and has the cultural gaps that Woody Allen had after he woke up in "Sleeper." Eric had never seen Seinfeld and doesn't understand the millions of Sienfeldian idioms that have become permanent in American usage. He is wonderful and very sophisticated in the European sense (speaks and understands several languages), but if you meet him, speak to him as if he were Mork from Ork. Don't be surprised if his eyes glaze over if you say "yadda yadda." He is studying and writing about Hannah Arendt. Talking about Hannah Arendt, if evil is banal as she said, then cancer is twice so. Banal, boring, and time-consuming. A total drag.

Suzanne and I spent four wonderful days in Santa Fe with my brother-in-law Ray and his too-good-to-be-true wife Wendy. We drove a convertible in the warm sunshine and the clean air, went on long hikes in the mountains, and had great and healthy macrobiotic meals. I met with a nutritionist who told me I could eat chicken, which I regarded as a major victory. But she otherwise ruled out every other food that I enjoy, including Cream of Wheat: that's right, good old blander-than-bland *Cream of Wheat,* which she regarded as allergenic for someone with A+ blood type. So much for nutrition. I'm sticking with Cream of Wheat. In Washington nearly everyone is a lawyer. In Santa Fe, nearly everyone is a naturopath, massage therapist, clairvoyant, spritualist, shaman, Zen meditator, or healer of some sort. While I was visiting there was a huge Ram Das celebration going on. You remember Ram Das (aka Richard Alper). The Guru before being a guru was cool. There is so much healing going on in Santa Fe that I was surprised anyone there is sick, but of course, that is not the case. There were large billboards advertising the soothing Santa Fe Cancer Center. Apparently neither Zen meditation nor the harmonic convergence can eradicate cancer. Hospital beds must be filled.

I'll keep you posted. Gabe is at basketball camp. Zak is in New York on a research assistantship. Shira, Russ, and Caleb are enjoying the summer. Caleb has spoken two full sentences. And my Suzanne is, well, perfect as ever.
Love to you all, Ned

PS. On Monday, July 7, my email address will change to gratefulned@xxx.

NEW YORK

ART THERAPY IS GOOD FOR ME

July 31, 2003

Dear Friends and Family,

Above is a picture I created while waiting in the Sloan-Kettering transplant clinic to see my doctor on July 29. An energetic and lovely "art therapist" named Sarah saw me in the waiting room as I was reviewing the multitudinous "Consent To Treat" documents and, seizing the opportunity, approached and amiably advised me that art was "good therapy" for cancer patients. Since Suzanne has conditioned me to do anything anyone says is "good for me," I immediately accepted Sarah's offer of pencil and paper and water colors and what you see above is one of the products. I have titled it simply "clinic." As you can see I am from the minimalist Non-Hodgkins Lymphoma School of artiste patients. In that small circle, I hope to create a Matthew Barney "Cremaster Cycle"-type stir. It would be wise for you to buy my art while the market is in creation, so to speak.

I was at S-K to meet with my doctor and undergo some tests to firmly establish that I am the great treatment paradox: a man with the right amount of cancer who is otherwise "healthy enough to survive the uncomfortable and longish immuno-depressive state that is part-and-parcel of the bone marrow transplant process." Naturally, I passed all tests with flying colors. I am that kind of man. The net result is that on August 4, I will enter S-K to begin chemo pre-treatment and, on Wednesday, August 13, will receive the stem cells of another living human being who replicates me hematologically as closely as possible for anyone not my exact twin. This is food for huge existential thought, but more about that later. You should know that in the transplant circles in which I now circulate, they speak of the actual transplant as being "born again" (to coin a phrase) and the transplant date as your new birth date. That being the case, I am asking that you save Sunday, August 15, 2004 for another Grateful Ned party, celebrating my new birthday, one year out from the you-know-what. No gifts please. [This party never took place.]

I have been told that my donor is a 50-year-old woman with children. My donor's profile immediately made me anxious that, once engrafted, I would slowly morph into a woman. My doctor says that won't be the case but I hope that you will all understand if I experience any gender confusion as a result of my transplant. To be on the safe side, if anyone out there has a pair of blue and white spectator pumps (two inch heels) save them for me. I hope I come back as a size 6-7.

Beginning August 4, I will be in reverse isolation in S-K hospital for four to six weeks. This means I will not be allowed out of my room and visitation will be controlled. I am required to be in New York for 100 days from August 13 until November 21. On that date, if things go well, I will be allowed to return to Washington to re-enter civilized

Random Thoughts on Patienthood

1. Never lie in the bed, take your chemo sitting up.
2. Illusion is that one's life is guaranteed until the bomb drops.
3. Not courageous: have no choice. Not given a choice.
4. Gradually dealing with the fear. Fear comes first. Nobody can stay fearless all the time. Must integrate the fear into your life rather then be ruled by it.
5. Although I have in all likelihood less time, I find myself acting as though I have more.
6. Visit to rheumatologist: Go out and live your life; had a secret inside of me.
7. Know the Score: Political correctness infects treatment too.
8. Cast Away
9. Don't be judgmental: Non-judgmental, everyone has a *shtick*.
10. Leave advice to the professionals. I had wonderfully experienced doctors at the M.D. Anderson Cancer Center in Houston, Texas, and in Washington, D.C. who developed and implemented the aggressive chemotherapy regimen that helped me gain remission from my lymphoma.
11. I had a wonderful t'ai chi instructor whose lessons about focus enabled me to get through some tough chemo sessions.
12. My family changed its diet dramatically so that I (and everyone) eat more nutritiously more consistently (even with some cheating).
13. I prayed regularly. (Couldn't get enough of Psalms.)

society, but will not be permitted to linger amidst large groups for a while longer. I will not be able to return to my work at the Department of Justice until about mid-January 2004.

Since I will be out of work for so much longer than anticipated, I would greatly appreciate any leave any Federal employee has to spare. I am an approved Leave Bank Recipient, not my greatest claim to fame.

I enter this phase of my life with no illusions, but with the expectation that it will be, as most things are, an unpredictable roller coaster ride for which I am as ready as I can be. In the last two years I have been the recipient of many prayers and other kindnesses. They have sustained me and my family.

Next year in Rock Creek Park.
Thank you, Ned Stutman

TRANSPLANT DIARY

August 3, 2003: Suzanne and I arrived in New York at 6:00 p.m. and observed a late model SAAB was magically about to depart a parking spot convenient to her sister's apartment. Suzanne and I waited patiently for the SAAB to alight the space and prepared to back in when a huge SUV with two huger guys tried to front end its way in. The SUV has guessed wrong, because the guy in the AUDI (me) was anyone's worst nightmare: a guy with a life-threatening illness who was about to undergo a heroic procedure and had nothing to lose. I confronted the SUV and after some heated words, the SUV thought better of it and left. I was victorious in my first skirmish in New York. My advice to anyone who would try to invade my space without the expressed written consent of the commissioner of the NFL: think better of it. I'm in no mood to mess around.

August 4: Check In. Suzanne and I reported for duty at Sloan-Kettering Hospital at 8:30 a.m. but the "OPF" (Office of Patient Finances) had not "cleared" my admission so it was delayed. Like the two guys in the SUV, I promptly confronted the "patient service representative" and advised that all the insurance piece of this had been worked out in advance. Unlike the parking space skirmish, this was a battle I was destined to lose. No treatment can start until the hospital is satisfied that the proper respect (read, bill) will be paid. The delay wasn't major, but any snafu at this point would have been annoying. For some reason, I am ready for a fight at a moment's notice. I decide to calm down. That resolve lasts until I found out that I had to pay for cable and that telephone service cost $6 per day. The patient care coordinator asks if I have a "living will" and is grateful that I do and brought a copy for them. It provides that if I am unable to do so, all medical decisions are to be made by my dog Scout.

I got admitted and was taken to a room. Because the whole floor was recently renovated, there was nothing hanging on the walls. The only "art" on the wall was a centigrade-fahrenheit conversion chart. An oncology nurse and trainee took 12 vials of blood. The trainee had never drawn blood from a Hickman catheter before and was nervous, and somewhat awkward, dripping blood on my bed. I didn't complain, but watched her carefully to make sure she didn't make any serious mistakes, like blowing 10 cc's of air into my aorta. I am now waiting for surgery to call me to replace my Seattle-placed double-lumen Hickman with a triple-lumen job — all the better to fill me to the brim with stuff. Surgery is not sure they will get to me today. Placement of this new catheter was, of course, the only reason I was admitted today and not tomorrow.

At about 5:00 p.m. I had my Seattle-installed left-mounted two-lumen catheter replaced by a longer sleeker three-lumen job. As I lay on the operating table, the doctor advised me that he didn't want to remove my Seattle-installed Hickman because he didn't like the way it was implanted. He said he would be glad to give me a new catheter on the right side. I didn't like having two body openings when one would do. He quickly relented (he was easier to convince than the SUV guys) since, he said, he loved my Sloan-Kettering doctor (Papadopoulos) and would do anything for her. They shot me up with Demerol and Versed and I was off to the races. I got back to my room at about 6:30 p.m. and continued to sleep through the night.

August 5: Treatment began in earnest. I received some chemo and then Campath, a monoclonal antibody. Campath is infused over six hours. Just as I had a reaction to the first installment of another monoclonal antibody in Houston (Rituxan), I had a reaction to the Campath. After about three hours, I developed chills and a high fever spike. Between Suzanne covering me like a blanket and imaging a warm beach and good nursing care including a shot or two of

Thoughts on Living Life to the Last Moment

WHAT HAPPENED FOR ME is that I knew I had a limited future, and so things changed.

Most people don't contemplate what the end of life is going to be like because you have this future which, while not certain, still seems to be more than just a possibility. However, for me I realized my time was limited. And things changed for the better in the sense that for the first time I was able to appreciate a moment that I was actually having. As I was growing up, my mother, may she rest in peace, only appreciated things in retrospect. During a party she'd be nervous, nervous, nervous, and then three weeks later she'd say "Wasn't that a nice party?" and so that was the way I was brought up. During any happy event, I would be nervous, and then later I'd say it was nice. Now Suzanne, my wife, has kind of knocked that out of me. She has taught me how to appreciate life, which was probably the main reason I married her. I knew she would do that.

But even more so, with the illness, I'm able to concentrate on a moment and see how nice it is at the time it is happening. Sitting at the dinner table with my two boys, holding my grand daughter or grandson — things that might not matter in the ordinary course of events, to me they're very meaningful. And I remember them all like they were major events where I invite 300 people. As a matter of fact, these unpredictable moments are the most important moments to me right now.

But I do still struggle with concepts like survivorship and what survivorship means. Life is full of experiences. In some respect, going to Fresh Fields [now Whole Foods] is an experience. And every day we have a multitude of experiences. Some experiences are more meaningful; certainly with this illness because it's such a major influence on you and your day to day existence, it kind of infiltrates and governs every aspect of your life.

Thoughts on being a "Survivor" I'm unwilling to recognize my illness as a force for positive change. There are some ways that I'm better now than I was before. As mentioned above, I'm much more attentive to my children. By virtue of all this stuff people have given me to read, I'm much more able to live in the moment. I recognize a moment when it happens. Many times you don't even recognize you're having a moment. Now I'm able to be in the moment more reliably than I have ever been able to do it. But, you know, I never thought of myself as a survivor. I've always felt that I was sort of interim. I was neither fish nor fowl. And when people would talk about cancer survivors, I would say to myself "Just wait." It always made me angry. Survivor is overused the way holocaust is overused. "Survivor" for me — as someone who was in the Justice Department hunting Nazis — "survivor" for me has a specialized meaning and I think the overuse of it trivializes it.

I also don't like it because it creates an artificial distinction between those who through luck or other things were able to hold the disease at bay longer than others. And so to say that someone who survived cancer should be elevated higher than someone who succumbed to the disease I think serves no useful purpose and it makes someone like me angry — someone who is facing constant battles. I feel like I'm very interim and my life has been very interim for four years.

Thoughts on Fears The other piece of it though is that I've been living with a kind of fear for this time and it's a funny kind of fear because it can be buried and you can pile stuff on top of it and walk around and nobody can actually see it but it's really there and it pops up in funny ways. It pops up when you get a pain in a place you've never gotten a pain before. If you get a fever, heaven forbid I get a low grade fever, my whole life changes for five days. That's just the way it is. I am a victim of every hospital protocol you can imagine. And so you have a fear that's always with you.

Demerol, we got it under control and I finished the course. It was not unexpected, but still felt lousy.

August 6: Second day of treatment. I received a unit of blood between the chemo and I am receiving the second six-hour installment of Campath as I write. As of three hours, no reaction yet.

STEM CELLS CAN BECOME ANYTHING THEY WANT TO BE

Ned's world view

August 9, 2003

Dear Family and Friends,

This is the 59th Street Bridge, as seen from my window. It connects Manhattan to Queens and was the bridge that titled the Simon and Garfunkel's '70s song "Feelin' Groovy" which I didn't appreciate much then, but do now. My East River view is beautiful. Sloan-Kettering places all transplant patients in double rooms since they are not permitted to leave their rooms during their "reverse isolation" period of six weeks. Reverse isolation means that everyone who enters my room must take infection precautions — wear gloves and a mask and later, a gown, but I do not have to. Because everyone's face is covered, I find myself reading peoples' eyes. I have discovered that eyes don't lie: a smile is a smile and concern is concern. Having worn a mask from time to time, I know how uncomfortable it can be. Try sucking on a napkin for an hour or two.

Things go well. I have had a week of chemo with the usual ups and downs but nothing that I couldn't manage. Zak is in New York living like a high-class vagabond. He spent two weeks in a swell Soho apartment of a brother of a dear friend, and just moved up to Central Park West where he occupies other swell digs of a generous friend of my indefatigable cousin, Lyn. Suzanne and Gabe are in East Hampton for the weekend with our trusty canine companion, Scout. Our living arrangements for the post-hospital stay period are still in formation.

I have chemo on Sunday and Monday, a day of rest, and then the stem cell transplant on Wednesday. Oddly enough, my exactly-matched donor is not my blood type (A+) so her stem cells will have to be filtered from her red cells before transfusion. My scientist brother Joel tells me that stem cells are cells that can become anything they want to be. This is a one-time and irrevocable decision for each of them. After the transplant, we just have to hope that enough of my new stem cells decide they want to be Ned Stutman. Knowing me as well as I do, I know this will be a difficult decision, and probably a big personal sacrifice for each of them. I just hope that I don't have to live with millions of stem cells carping: "Look what I gave up to be you!!" What would you decide? Enough said.

Judaism has a blessing for every conceivable occasion, but I don't know if there is one for this fairly unique life cycle event. So if you can, think of a blessing of thanksgiving for receiving someone else's stem cells or blood, and send it to me. I will entertain blessings from any religious tradition; my only preference is that it invoke the universal deity. Sorry, but I must draw the line at idol worship, wicca, consorting with spirits, or anything having to do with the Osbornes.
Love to all, Ned

STROLLING ON YORK AVENUE I DON'T THINK ABOUT TOMORROW

September 26, 2003

"May you be inscribed..."

For a year in which you are mindful of, and value, the love, beauty, and inspiration that will come your way.

Although Rosh Hashanah is upon us, I am in a Shavuot state of mind. Shavuot (Heb. lit.: "weeks") is an important (if not widely observed) Jewish Holiday that typically falls in early June, exactly 50 days after the Spring holiday of Passover. It commemorates, among other things, the giving of the 10 Commandments (and more) to the newly-freed Hebrew slaves at Mt. Sinai. So important is this holiday that, as a prelude, Jews are commanded by the Hebrew Bible to explicitly and expressly count each of the 49 days between the end of Passover, and the beginning of Shavuot. By way of example the formula is, thus: "Today is 43 days, which are six weeks and one day, of the Omer." The "Omer" is a special grain offering that was made at Passover. Hence the practice of counting each of the 49 days is called "counting the Omer." It is not an easy thing to do and if you miss a night, hard-nosed tradition forbids you to carry on the count. I have tried and failed more than once. Anyway, I tell you this because I think that "counting days" can add an important element to High Holiday observance, even as Rosh Hashanah seems so directed at the gestalt of the coming year and is replete with figurative imagery.

By way of explanation, on September 23 I was released after 40 days of isolation in the Sloan-Kettering Bone Marrow Transplant Center. On August 13, to the sounds of *Adon Olam* sung by my Suzanne and children, and the recital of various original prayers composed by family and friends, and while holding my teffilin (I couldn't possibly explain this term: "phylactories" doesn't help much) I had received the stem cells of a 50-year-old woman whom I may never meet but who may have saved my life. Post-transplant, I am required to be in shouting distance of S-K for 100 days from August 14, i.e., until November 23. During my pre- and post-transplant period, doctors and pathologists pour over my own numbers: red and white cells, platelets, and at least 40 other indicators of how I am doing. A tenth of a degree centigrade

If Cancer is a Gift, Where Can I Find Customer Service?

ONE THING I HEAR OVER AND OVER AGAIN from cancer veterans is how cancer is a force for change, positive change in their lives. Some even call it a "gift." Before cancer they were one person. After a bout with the disease they were another and demonstrably better version of themselves. More loving, less impatient, living in more mindful ways. Allied with this message was the literary metaphor that a bout with cancer was a "journey" as in a period of symbolic as well as actual struggle and learning, such as experienced by the Man of LaMancha. Or even better, cancer is a turning point, as in my life had been going in the non-spiritual, materialistic direction for a long time and cancer gave me a much-needed goose to reorient myself toward what was really important. I have had a naturopath tell me that I got cancer for a reason and now that I am living differently I don't need the disease anymore and should try to find a way to get rid of it. Now there's good advice!

Well *if cancer is a journey I should have asked for directions.* Moreover the "we are all in the same boat" mentality doesn't work for me because I have no intention of traveling. When I was diagnosed, I was about to begin a very important Federal trial I had prepared for three years, and thinking about retirement a couple years later. Getting diagnosed felt like a bomb was dropped on my life. It was only later that I saw the sitcom potential in it.

often separated sleep from a frenzy of activity to monitor a possible infection. I hit 38 degrees every so often and had the pleasure of a road trip to the X-ray room, often in the middle of the night to avoid other people. These high-speed wheelchair forays were the highlight of my isolation.

And so, each night before I go to sleep, I count my personal Omer. For your information, tonight, using the ancient formula I will say:

"Today is 43 days, which are six weeks and one day of my Omer." And what a beautiful day it was. The weather was perfect. In the morning, together with my beloved mother-in-law roommate-for-a-day Rose, I walked to S-K for some blood work and examination. My counts turned out to be very good. (For my doctors out there: WBC: 10.6, Hgb: 9.5, Plat. 369,000, ANC: 8.8.) I had a wonderful lunch with Mom and my sister-in-law Bonnie, and then later, after a full and delicious meal prepared under the auspices of my cousins Lyn and George, my Suzanne and I took an equally delicious stroll down York Ave. I don't think about tomorrow. Who knows what it will bring and for me, right now, it doesn't matter.

As you have seen, I have avoided the traditional Rosh Hashanah greeting: "May you be inscribed for a sweet New Year." It is a warm and friendly sentiment, but only that, a sentiment. It doesn't reflect the reality of people's lives much, and gives a fantastic if traditional folk image of how life works in the world. The truth is that "sweetness" and a good year are for each of us to see and know when we have it. Life is full of ups and downs, some quite consuming and serious. Each of us would be better served to wish that another recognize and count each day and the loving moments it has brought. This I have been trying to do and believe me, like counting the Omer, it is not an easy thing to do. It takes practice.

My new address is: The Helmsley ("only little people pay taxes") Medical Towers Building.

Finally, I apologize for any offense I may have committed against any of you and ask for forgiveness. I forgive everyone.
Love, Ned

MY TRANSPLANT TEAM – "HOPE" AND "BLESSING"
October 18, 2003
Dear Family and Friends,
Here is a photo of me and my "transplant team." I am second from the right. These clowns spend a lot of time in the pediatric unit at Sloan-Kettering, and immediately recognized a kindred spirit. They recruited

Clowning around at Sloan-Kettering

me for the holiday party at which time I will do eight minutes of stand-up. I have not settled on a theme but am considering: "Take my cancer! Please!" or "Ned, (STILL) LIVE at Sloan-Kettering!" [As far as we know, Ned never did this.]

I can confirm that laughter is especially good therapy for people with cancer. I don't know if there are hard data to support this view, but no matter. Whereas FDA-approved drugs have to be proven both safe and effective, it's enough for me that laughter is safe. I take humor very seriously. It is an integral and, if you ask me, the best part of my personality. In 1990 I won a real comedy club competition for the Funniest Lawyer in Washington. Heavy is the head that wears that crown, believe me. But I must tell you that while most of my life is a blur, among a few moments, I remember my nine minutes of stand-up with crystalline clarity — every gesture, every laugh, every hiss (just a few), everything. Those nine minutes were some of the happiest of my life. But, because I am a serious amateur comedian, I am also a tough audience. I tend to be clinically analytical about humor.

Humor between cancer veterans is sometimes a dark coded private communication in a secret language containing code words and images shared only between and among the initiated, those who would understand and appreciate the irony of humor in their often tentative situations. Some of the best jokes I heard (ever) I heard in clinic.

The real head of my transplant team is pictured here. She is on the right. Her name is Esperanza Papadopoulos, MD. Esperanza means "hope." One of the Fellows assisting her is named Boruchov, which

Top Ten Pluses from Getting Cancer

Cancer treatment is not the least bit funny, but it does have its ironic aspects. Some positives about getting cancer:

1. Getting cancer eliminated the worry about getting cancer

2. From the day I was diagnosed in July 2001 to this very weekend, on every Shabbat a friend delivered a home-baked super delicious challah. We all look forward to this challah and it has taken on a life of its own.

3. My salt and pepper hair, lost during chemo, reappeared darker and thicker.

4. Chemo improved my singing voice.

5. My photographs were of much higher quality, since chemo improved my vision of the world and people in it.

6. The Department of Justice gave me a parking space.

7. For more than three years, I was privileged to see on a consistent basis and almost exclusively the generous and compassionate side of human beings. This would include not only close family, extended family and friends, but acquaintances, friends of friends, people with whom I had been accidentally or purposefully awkward, people who I had avoided out of shyness, embarrassment, fear or contempt. Everyone in my universe seemed

means "blessing." Having a team of "hope" and "blessing" may help explain why I chose Sloan-Kettering.

I must admit that I lapsed in my daily counting of each of the 100 days from my transplant (August 13), to my anticipated release date

Ned and Dr. Papadopoulos

genuinely interested in my fight and my progress and virtually all gave me something to ease the way.

8. Cancer taught me "mindfulness" (which is probably some swami's service mark). It made me more aware of "the moment" and more capable of enjoying it. Cancer made me more interested in others; more patient in listening, more capable of enjoying a moment. This was not easy to do since one of the side effects of chemo is a kind of ADD which makes it harder to concentrate on anything more complicated than buttoning your shirt.

9. Cancer took over the job of killing me that my day to day work as government-sponsored Nazi hunter had occupied. WHAT A RELIEF! As a Senior Trial Attorney in the United States Department of Justice, I hunted Nazi persecutors who were ineligible for immigration but had nonetheless secured U.S. citizenship after WWII. It was chronically saddening work, more so as I realized how little people cared about the fate of Jewish victims, how little they care now, and how little has changed internationally since 1945. Cancer gave me the time and inclination to explore my spiritual and creative self or, put another way, to create a spiritual self.

10. Chemo cured my psoriasis.

(November 23). Baseball fans will appreciate that I failed to count day 55, one day short of 56. Now I know exactly how hard it is to break Joe DiMaggio's 56 consecutive game hitting record.

Regarding my clinical picture, as my grandmother might say to avoid the evil eye, "it could be worse." I feel a little like the old Jewish man who is hit by a car while crossing a street. A concerned pedestrian rushes to the old man's side, covers him, and asks "Are you comfortable?" to which the old man replies "I make a living." Actually, all my gauges are centered and vital bodily fluids which are dipsticked regularly seem to be just right. Yesterday I visited Sotheby's in full battle gear (mask and latex gloves) to view exhibited photographs. Today I had lunch at an outdoor cafe. One little boy asked Suzanne if I had SARS. Even though I may be nearing Purity of Essence as General Jack the Ripper might say,

I am slow to allow thoughts of complete normalcy for me, my family, and friends. Such reluctance is a natural if unfortunate result of stereotypical Jewish folk tradition as well as the curse of prolonged health uncertainty. My key phrase remains, "we'll see."

For those of you keeping score today is day 66 of the 100 days.

Love, Ned

Ned takes on New York

WASHINGTON

HOLDING HANDS FOR A HUNDRED MILES

November 2, 2003

Dear Family and Friends,

On Tuesday my doctor found me "rehabilitated," gave me time off for good behavior and told me I could go home. I returned to Washington on Saturday, Nov. 1, which corresponds to day 80 of my 100-day count.

Unfortunately, I returned to a non-functioning kitchen since, while I was in treatment, Suzanne was forced to undertake some long-needed and essential repairs which have not been completed. I have therefore been required to take refuge for a few days in Chevy Chase's re-knowned Hotel Epstein (you can always check in but you can never leave — without saying grace after meals), enjoying the hospitality of America's Concierge Ellen (brisket and chicken for breakfast — no problem) Epstein and the intellectual stimulation of her husband David. David has been feeding me interesting tidbits from a biography of John Adams that he has recently read. (Example: Did you know that Adams was a bare bones entertainer, unlike Jefferson who was lavish in every way?)

My donated and my newly-acquired woman's intuition failed me and I was totally taken aback by news of my early release. I certainly knew I was ready to come home. Just last week, I asked Suzanne to put my dog Scout on the telephone. (Scout held up his end of the conversation quite well. He is, after all, an ENGLISH Springer Spaniel.) Although not many transplant patients get early release, I am keenly aware that I am still being watched and I will have more tests at or around day 100. Many of my clinical markers are good and holding, but I still have a suppressed immune system which will take some time to recover. My hair is coming back; I look fine and feel stronger every day. I weigh 156 lbs., my pre-diagnosis running weight. But doctors rely on "the data" which still mark me as vulnerable. I have a thousand and one hygiene and food prep rules to follow. I must wear a mask outside to protect against fungus that accompanies fall foliage, however beautiful it may be. I must be cautious about physical contact which is completely contrary to my temperament. I am a "hugger" — and am bereft that my real, imagined, and perceived vulnerability inhibits me from embracing and kissing the people I care about.

The mask is a little freaky and makes people reluctant to come near. Kids stare. The knowledge that all this will pass does little to reduce my feeling of isolation.

Whatever. My complaints are the smallest of potatoes. As I was driven home, Suzanne and I held hands for 100 miles. We ushered that Sabbath out with friends in a moment of warmth and gratitude. I silently thanked God for separating the day from the night of my life in the most literal way. My homecoming coincided with Gabe's 16th birthday and added a special note of celebration. We just learned that Shira is pregnant with a girl who, we pray, will join us in March. The autumn is inestimably beautiful, even if my mask prevents me from savoring its aroma. I am grateful to enjoy it. Life is good.

I entered summer camp at Sloan-Kettering with no expectations — only serious curiosity and hopes. My curiosity has been more than satisfied and my hopes have been more than realized, at least for the time being which is, after all, all there is.

The words "thank you" seem so pathetically inadequate to express the appreciation I feel for all that you all have done for me and my family during the last five months, but it's all there is.
More later. Love, Ned

What I always say is what I want to do up to the very end is same old, same old. I don't want a trip to Disney World; I don't want to go to Venice or Florence although I'd love to see them. Routine is what I really like. I love the people I work with. I love the work I'm doing. Being with my nuclear family and my extended family, if I can do that, is all that I ask for at this point. If I can get up in the morning and make the bed then I'm very, very happy. I really never set higher objectives for myself than that.

NEW SHIRTS AND SLACKS TO CELEBRATE GOING BACK TO WORK

February 8, 2004

Dear Family and Friends,

Tomorrow, February 9, almost exactly six months after my stem cell transplant, I go back to work in the Department of Justice. To celebrate, I went shopping and bought two new shirts and a pair of slacks (I am now a 34 inch waist, down from 36) for the occasion. I got my new black hair cut after arguing with my barber on how it should be styled. He wanted a number-two-blade short cut. My hair took so long to come back that I decided to leave it longish. I bought a tube of Alberto VO5. Hair care is now an issue.

I will be returning to the Civil Rights Division (CRD) where I worked in DOJ years ago, and still have many friends of long standing. I leave the Office of Special Investigations with nothing but affection for my friends/colleagues there, and gratitude for the sacrifices they made without complaint in my absence. At this time I simply could not assume my old litigation practice with all its necessities. I am forever indebted to all my colleagues in the Criminal Division, including those in Administration who guided me through the morass of rules that apply to someone in my situation. I am excited to go back to CRD which quickly made room for me and where many of the issues I dealt with years ago still seem to resonate, although in different forms.

As for all of you, thank you for everything you gave, and sacrifices you made that allowed me and my family to reach this day. It would be impossible to recognize individuals because so many contributed so much and I know any

Hanging at the
Library of Congress

listing would inevitably leave someone out (as most Academy Award recipients find out, usually the hard way). But you should know that I was the beneficiary of stem cells, blood and platelets, love, annual leave, accommodations for me and my family, kitchen remodeling, air travel, limousine service, vacations, food (entire meals for six), Shabbat challahs, transportation and all manner of sustenance for Gabe, dog-walking, prayers of all persuasions, hospital visits, massages and reflexology, get well wishes, words of wisdom, amulets, books, audio and video tapes, clothes, and other kindnesses unimaginable in both kind and amount. (I have been advised that the amount of leave donated established — by far — some sort of record in the Department.) In retrospect, it seems that my life as a sick man was much more luxurious than my life as a well man. Even so, I am ready to resume my former existence, even if it means cooking and cleaning up. I think my family is ready too. For now, for me, nothing seems more luxurious than returning to same old, same old.

So, hopefully and regretfully, I sign off. I have decent blood counts and have weathered some of the squalls that come without notice on the post-transplant seas. I get treatment for some issues from time to time, still take things day by day, and try to remember my worst treatment days whenever I am seduced to anger or impatience.
Ned

P.S. I am now ineligible for any more leave donations. All leave donated to me and not used will be returned to the donors.

YOUR STEM CELLS GAVE ME SIX MONTHS AND COUNTING

[written to Ned's unknown bone marrow donor]
June 11, 2004
Dear "Perfect Stranger,"
I write on June 11, 2004, ten months after my transplant, to thank you for your gift. I received your pinkish-strawberry-slurpy-like stem cells on August 13, 2003. At the time I was 58. I am now 59. At the time I had one grandson. I now have seen a new granddaughter. I owe achieving these milestones to you, since your generosity has given me ten

months and counting. Your stem cells were
infused over a period of eighteen minutes;
a short time considering. During those
eighteen minutes, my wife, my 30-year-old
daughter, my 16-year-old son and I sang
some songs and read prayers that were
prepared by friends just for this unique
life cycle event. The infusion was fairly
straightforward and clinical; but the event
itself became highly spiritual. You were
there in our hearts. We gave you a name
by which we would know you.

Ned snuggles with
granddaughter Maya

I can tell you that I also have a 25-year-old son who is in graduate
school. My daughter is studying to be a Rabbi, is married to a talented
educator, and together they have a son two-and-three-quarter years
old and a daughter three months old. My wife is a beautiful, strong,
intelligent, and professional woman of 58 who has been my bedrock
during treatment. As of February 9, 2004, I have been back at work on
a reduced schedule — about thirty hours per week. I feel like I am doing
fine, although as you can imagine, the post-transplant period is full of
mini-crises that instantly mobilize a cast of thousands. I am thankful for
every day and don't worry much about the future since, for each of us,
it is uncertain. I consider your act perfect in every respect. I know that
the act of donation itself is time-consuming, typically inconvenient and
uncomfortable. Speaking from experience, I know that nobody likes to
get stuck by needles when they don't have to.

My religious belief system counts as the most perfect act of charity
one when neither the donor nor the recipient know the other's
identity. Every day of my life I am aware that I am now related to you,
a stranger who made a perfect act of charity to me. You are, then,
a "perfect stranger," in the most literal meaning of that phrase. I can
never repay your generosity one for one, but I hope to be able to
thank you enough and in the right way that you will never have any
doubts whatsoever.

APRIL 6, 2005
Ned's 60th Birthday Party: Payback Time

Ned with friend Janet Waxman and cousin Lyn Ross

Dearest friends and family:

With thanks to God and Her workers here on earth, and against all odds, Ned Stutman will have his 60th birthday in just a few weeks (April 6). In honor of his birthday, we are putting together a book of photos and comments — and we'd like you to be a part of it.

We know you're all busy, but hope that you can take a few minutes to write a few, short lines. Specifically, we're looking for Ned-related anecdotes. Nothing too heavy or poignant, please; on his birthday this year, the still reigning "Funniest Lawyer in Washington" wants to spend a lot of time laughing.

Shhhhh... it's a surprise!!!!! Send your comments, if and when you have them, to shiras@xxx. And, PLEASE forward this email to anyone else you think may have something to say.

For all of you who have ever been teased, ribbed, or otherwise tickled (literally or metaphorically) by our dad – it's payback time. We look forward to hearing from you soon.

With love, the Stut/Stut-Shaw kids

Right: Ned's children
Shira Stutman-Shaw,
Zak and Gabe Stutman

Below: Friend
Ellen Epstein
and son-in-law
Russ Shaw

Mother-in-law
Rose Singer,
sister-in-law
Bonnie Jacobson,
brother-in-law
Ray Singer,
wife Suzanne
and Ned

SUDDEN RETIREMENT, LIKE HITTING THE DELETE BUTTON

July 13, 2005

Dear Family and Friends,

I haven't written for a while because for the better part of 2004 and despite some treatment zigs and zags, my day to day life had settled into a wonderfully satisfying routine. Although I was nearly always receiving one miracle treatment or the other (FYI: Thalidomide is back), I had a particularly rewarding year. Among other things, my work in the Coordination and Review Section of DOJ's Civil Rights Division was enriching. My colleagues there (as they were in OSI) were, by

---

Not Making the Grade but Still Finding the Humor

IT'S INTERESTING, AS TIME HAS GONE ON… I realize there have always been disappointments. I've never gotten an F but I usually, since the very beginning, got C pluses, maybe B minus the first time, but my treatments have never been particularly efficacious, and that even goes for my stem cell transplant. I would call it a "C"; it was only minimally successful. I don't expect an A tomorrow. I would be shocked if my doctor said "we're making tremendous progress with this medication. We're going to keep you on this medication, and we think that we're going to put you in remission."

I don't have any feelings of resentment against any of my medical professionals. Each one has been very competent. I just think it is what it is. This is a nasty kind of cancer.

My humor has stayed intact. Every so often I lose it because I find that I'm not well enough. But most of the time if my mind is strong, my humor is still there. It has to do with how agile my mind is. Humor has always helped me, because humor, for me, is just another perspective on the world. Ironies abound, and to observe these ironies is wonderful. There are incredibly funny stories that emerge from cancer treatment and the cancer world and the way

themselves, life sustaining not to mention life enhancing. In addition, I shopped, cooked, caught some of Gabe's basketball games, went to the movies, enjoyed family and friends, and for the most part, did what normal people do. It was a sweet time, if too short.

On April 1, 2005 I retired from federal service after 25 years. Some people retire; others have retirement thrust upon them. Retirement came to me suddenly and, despite everything, unexpectedly. A series of minor treatment aftershocks sent me to the hospital seriatim in late November and December 2004. My increasingly frequent and unpredictable three- or four-day absences from the office were making

they do business in these cancer hospitals. My humor is always born out of exposing the ironies in the world. People laugh when they see it and when they hear it.

However, I will tell you — and I'm embarrassed to admit this — I never brought any anger to bear in my fight. I never thought of this as a battle I was in, in the sense that I was just never angry about it, as in "why me?" I did whatever was required of me. I was a good soldier. I never complained. But I didn't have a sense of resentment or failure in terms of myself either. I didn't think of myself that way. I saw it in a clinical way. I was interested in the clinical aspect of it and I tried to learn about it. But I often wonder about myself. You read about people, who talk about their fight, and they fought this and they fought that … even Lance Armstrong when you read his book, it's really about his aggression. They bring all their aggression to bear. My approach has been different. It hasn't been a clear-cut feeling of aggression that I would bring as a lawyer to a fight defending a client. I don't think that kind of aggression is at my core. I think I'm much more of a cooperative, congenial person than someone who's always trying to be number one. I often wonder whether I hurt myself by not approaching it that way.

Sharing a laugh with Zak while getting ready for a party, 1998

it hard for me, my supervisors and my colleagues. I felt I had to face hard facts. My illness was taking up too much work time. With no plan, I retired.

Of course I now realize how central my work was to my identity and how suddenly retiring was like accidentally hitting the delete button eliminating a major project. I took pride in the work I did as a DOJ attorney and was, in part, defined by it. Now I am no longer "Ned the civil rights lawyer" or "Ned the Nazi hunter." I have settled on calling myself: "The DOJ attorney formerly known as Ned." I still have a hard time writing "retired" on all those forms that call for "Employer." However, I am still the reigning and champion Funniest Lawyer in Washington. Retirement hasn't changed that.

As for my daily routine: doctors, tests, and whatnot consume roughly 25-30% of my time. I am back in chemo as a prelude to obtaining immune cells from from my original donor who has stepped up to the plate for me again. We'll see how that goes. I have a million and one little complications that my doctors deal with as "collateral damage" on a first-come-first-served basis. All my doctors are endlessly confident about their skills and hopeful for me.

Despite the slings and arrows, I have, nevertheless, settled into something of a routine. In the morning I work on a book I am writing describing my experiences over the last four years. It is less a clinical account and more a "Tuesdays with Morrie"-style travelogue about the people I have met, the places I have been, and the inordinate kindnesses I have received. I have an email organizer, editor, and an agent (in N.Y.) who has submitted a proposal to a publisher. I am told that my agent "likes my voice." We'll see where my voice takes me. Publishers are notoriously unsentimental.

In my retirement I am even more sensitive to nature. All of a sudden I have discovered birds. I am awakened each day by an unseen woodpecker who has taken up residence in my neighborhood. I actually went looking for him (her?) but couldn't tell where the pecking sound was coming from. There is a beautiful cardinal that flies by my window every so often. The red bird is supposed to be lucky. My son-in-law got me a copy of the Audubon Guide to birds of the Northeast. I read it.

My family prospers despite what we call "the situation." Life remains good.
All the best, Ned

To God's kind hand
        I pledge my soul
each time I sleep,
        again to wake,
and with my soul,
        this body, here.
Adonai's love is mine;
        I shall not fear.

בְּיָדוֹ אַפְקִיד רוּחִי
בְּעֵת אִישַׁן וְאָעִירָה

וְעִם רוּחִי גְוִיָּתִי
יְהֹוָה לִי וְלֹא אִירָא׃

THOUGHTS ON RELIGION, PRAYER AND SPIRITUALITY IN HEALING

A MIND IS A HORRIBLE THING TO WASTE, and so during my years of cancer treatments, my wife and many of my friends set about trying to find ways to pry my mind open to look at the overall beauty in the universe in a very different way. While not rejecting, I must confess that I was not immediately open to new and different non-material — aka spiritual — and decidedly non-medical approaches to illness, or, as "they" put it: "wellness." I mean, face facts: What could chard or collard greens or acupuncture do that six rounds of the strongest chemo designed by medical science couldn't do?

However, even a pragmatic cynic can, occasionally, venture forth and experience new things. Primarily because I love my wife and trust her judgment, I became open to a whole host of what is known in the cancer biz as "Complementary and Alternative Medicine (CAM)."

And it is *really big* business. It includes such standards as acupuncture, holistic (naturopathic) medicine, organic and balanced nutrition, guided imagery. There are CAM practitioners of every stripe throughout the country; they hold meetings and conventions. The National Cancer Institute has even been required to start a CAM section and participate in selected clinical trials. Reike, healing touch, acupuncture, t'ai chi, yoga, aroma therapy — I've tried them all. When you have a life-threatening disease, sooner or later you set the mumbo-jumbo-limbo bar very high.

Religion

They say that there are no atheists in foxholes. That goes double for cancer hospitals. Like many life crises, serious illness both challenges the foundation of faith and creates a powerful need to believe that there is, in fact, something in control.

Pre-diagnosis, I was a mildly religious but completely non-spiritual person. I viewed Jewish prayer as a kind of group travel on the American Plan, since 1) it was usually costly, and 2) you had a guide at all times, and 3) food was always included. For many Jews, including me, Judaism is not "faith based," but rather "activity based" — in other words, you are a Jew because of what you do (as in what you eat), rather than what you believe. As a matter of fact, most Rabbis do not speak much of "faith," but exhort congregants to fulfill the commandments in the Hebrew Bible as the path to self-improvement and holiness. If you live life performing approved and time tested Bible-based deeds (*mitzvot*), so it goes, everything else will take care of itself.

The net result was that when I needed a spiritual anchor, I had none handy. I subsequently found out that there were many possibilities, including some I would have scoffed at pre-illness. I have come to believe that there is a whole world, a world of spiritual energy, that we cannot see or experience at the level of consciousness at which we operate in the material world. I am not embarrassed to say this. I scoff at nothing now.

But to begin. All cancer centers make room for the religious and spiritual needs of their patients. All have chapels and quiet spaces that get a lot of traffic. The visitors' books in such places are filled with beautiful and inspirational personal prayers, messages, and heartfelt expressions of sorrow and gratitude. The chapel in the Fred Hutchinson Cancer Center was the most eclectic, serving the spiritual needs of the big three as well as every other conceivable belief system including, as you might expect, Aleut, Native American, and Asian (of every stripe). I spent time in that chapel pulling "messages" in the form of Japanese origami swans out of the large wooden "blessing bowl." They were a little like cookie fortunes but you never got one that said "you will enjoy good health," and there were no lucky numbers.

M.D. Anderson's chapel was very Texas and very Christian in orientation. There were no Jewish prayer books.

Georgetown had a (removable) crucifix in every room which featured a figurine of a Jesus who looked like he was on steroids. Georgetown also had a permanent TV channel which broadcast live Mass regularly. I watched on occasion. (Georgetown is, after all, affiliated with the Catholic Church.) The Cortisone Jesus, however, stayed in my drawer. Without question, however, the most spiritual and reverential space I experienced was the famed Mark Rothko Chapel in Houston, about which you've read.

Upon admission to a cancer center, right after you are asked about whether you have a "Living Will" and "Final Instructions," patients are called upon to declare their "religious preference." I had never given any serious thought to whether I would "prefer" any religion other than that of my birth, Judaism. Given my travels, I had chances to jump my Jewish ship at each of the five institutions that treated me. Each time I ran through all the possibilities. Rastafarianism seemed exotic. I loved the dreadlocks even though the look was totally impossible with my post-chemo bald head. Also, I don't care for jerk chicken. I've always been secretly envious of Christians (Catholics, really): their services and the road to salvation are short and direct. Buddhism was a close call. It is long on spirituality and personal con- sciousness-raising which I wanted. But alas, it has as a core belief, the notion that enlightenment can only be achieved through suffering, although the idea that my and my family's suffering had some higher purpose was appealing. Islam interested me but I knew that I would have to learn another language which, like Hebrew, has its own script. I also was tired of dietary restrictions. It was impossible for me to consider any religion that included idol or nature worship. Thus some Native American and Alaskan belief systems were out. Wicca didn't make the short list. The bottom line: Time and again I stuck with Judaism. I just had too many other major decisions and felt that maybe this wasn't such a good time for such a fundamental change.

Having "declared" your religion, you were immediately targeted for pastoral counseling by hospital clergy of your "persuasion," most of whom are retired clergy. Visiting the sick is one of the three most highly regarded "good deeds" in Judaism. I would guess that it is the same in every religious belief system in the world except those that still practice human sacrifice. It is so valued because often the sick person can't thank you, and the act itself is a profoundly hard thing to do, especially if the patient has a serious illness.

While getting treatment as an inpatient, I looked terrible, was always in a semi-daze from some sort of toxic chemical being pumped into me and, more often than not, had no predictable or sustainable capability to interact on a human level with anyone other than my wife or close family who were prepared to tolerate me. I certainly wasn't in the mood to share how "I felt" with new people who were strangers to me. It was in this context that brave clergy valiantly tried to interact with me. In the end, I got more than I deserved from all of them, including some great material.

One 75-year-old Rabbi arrived, unannounced, and entered my room one day while I was getting some nasty treatment. (My treatment was almost as nasty as my disease.) He was in a rumpled suit and physically resembled the late borsht belt comic Buddy Hackett which immediately made me both playful and competitive. The brief conversation went as follows:

Rabbi: (Looking down at computer printout) Are you Mr. Stuntman?

Me: That's "Stutman" and yes I am.

Rabbi: Vel Mr. Stutman. I am Rabbi So-and-So. What are you doing here?

Me: Well Rabbi, I have cancer and this is a cancer hospital.

Then, assuming, zero knowledge on my part as Rabbis often do:

Rabbi: "Do you know that [the judgment days] of Rosh Hashanah and Yom Kippur are coming?

Me: Yes, I do.

Rabbi: Is there anything you want to say to me?

Me: Yes Rabbi, there is. Would you please pass me the apple juice?

Rabbi: Is there anything else I can do for you?

Me: Yes Rabbi. Take my cancer, please!

And with that, he was gone, promising to return, which he did. Things are improving, I thought. I now had a straight man for as long as I was in that hospital.

This same hospital had a "lay Jewish counselor" who was sponsored by a local Jewish organization. She tracked me down in clinic and offered to perform a service which, for lack of better term, I will call a "healing meditation." This woman had access to the hospital's newly opened "Complementary Medicine Center," which offered t'ai chi, yoga, and meditation. Her "healing meditation" turned out to be an hour of quiet, with the soft sounds of New Age-y music. Each session began with a Jewish prayer which I liked, since it brought me back into a familiar religious world. Then the woman would move her hands around my body without touching me. I found this relaxing and had several sessions. It was my one "treatment" that didn't leave me nauseated, sedated, stuck for a blood draw, drinking barium, or having a number five knitting needle stuck in my pelvis to aspirate bone marrow. I was disappointed when the woman declined to meet with me in my hospital room on a Sunday when I was sick as a dog from chemo, explaining simply "I don't work on Sundays." What a pity, I responded, since my chemo worked 24/7. As a person and a cancer patient I demanded more than knowledge and attention from my health care providers; I worked towards and demanded love and real connection. If neither was forthcoming, there was a problem. I never called her again.

In another hospital, a local Rabbi brought electric candlesticks to "kindle" on Friday nights and usher in the Jewish Sabbath. This Rabbi was of the "Conservative" Jewish denomination and offered to get my family tickets to upcoming High Holiday services. Committing a faux pas of epic proportions, I excitedly asked if he could get tickets to this wonderful local synagogue that I had visited frequently. The Rabbi was not, however, of that denomination, and well, it was as if I had asked a Mets fan for Yankees tickets. I thought the Rabbi was going to take back the candlesticks.

The Rabbi in Seattle was a woman who had been trained in yet another Jewish denomination — the "Jewish Renewal Movement." Founded by Rabbi and philosopher Zalman Schachter Shalomi, Jewish Renewal is "New Age Judaism" — heavily influenced by the spirituality that predominates in eastern religious thought. It also has elements of Chasidic Judaism, which calls upon Jews to experience transcendent religious joy through song. The Renewal Movement is light on adherence to Jewish law which, at that time, was just fine with me. "Cancer Ned" had a million self-care rules and dietary restrictions. "Cancer Ned" wasn't in the mood for any more restrictions. To her credit, this Rabbi actually tried to get me into spirituality and self-examination, providing me with tapes of the popular (in cancer circles) book, *Cancer as a Turning Point*. As the toaster is to newlyweds, this book is to cancer patients. I have been given five copies. My first reaction was cynicism: if cancer is a turning point, I should have asked for directions. I could foresee nothing positive coming out of this illness for either me, my family, or my friends. I was wrong.

Prayer

I USED TO BE AMBIVALENT about praying for good or improved health of a loved one. Of course it didn't stop me from doing it on the "what can it hurt" principle. It is also beneficial for the prayee. But praying for healing is tricky. For one thing, Jews are not permitted to pray for miracles. We are permitted to accept them, just not ask for them. From the beginning, I thought it would take a village of miracles to defeat my particularly nasty cancer but knew it would be cheeky to ask to send one. No, this would have to be His idea. Moreover, the idea that God would cure my illness seemed to accept, at least inferentially, the notion that He/She was responsible for the illness in the first place. It also accepted the idea that, being all-powerful, God could heal anyone at any time which, based on my experience, I could not fully accept.

Instead, I adopted Rabbi Harold Kushner's idea (from his book, *When Bad Things Happen to Good People*) that it is better to understand God as all good but not all powerful, rather than as an all powerful God that is not all good. À la Kushner, I came to understand my illness as a case of bad luck in a chaotic world of random events. This is decidedly not a traditional Jewish view, but somebody has to be a statistic and there was no reason why it shouldn't be me. I believe in luck. For good luck, I wear a red string around my wrist that rested on the tomb of the matriarch Rachel in Israel. Thus, I never asked "why me." Why not me? So, in the beginning, as with so many things, I didn't see the value of prayer.

I learned.

Data show that when their health is problematic, people pray and have others pray for them and their health improves. Curiously, classifying prayer, like folk medicine and hypnosis, as a "complementary" or "alternative" medical practice, the National Center for Complementary and Alternative Medicine (CAM) reported that 67% of Americans with a health condition either prayed for themselves or had others pray for them.[*] Why do so many people resort to prayer? Maybe because it works.

---

[*] Barnes P, Powell-Griner E, McFann K, Nahin R. CDC Advance Data Report #343. Complementary and alternative medicine use among adults: United States, 2002 May 27, 2004.

By now everyone is aware of a study that showed how a group of cardiac patients who, unbeknownst to them, had people praying for them, improved at a greater rate than another group of cardiac patients without prayers. Throughout my illness I had (and still have) legions of people praying for me. Jews have a special prayer that asks to deliver a complete healing to sick members of the community whose names are announced on Sabbath morning at the time Hebrew scripture is read. Thus, each Saturday morning, my name was said aloud in countless temples here and abroad, many unknown to me. I imagined a surge of energy every Saturday afternoon, which I attributed to these prayers. Catholics lit candles for me. A Shaman wanted a piece of my clothing to incorporate into some sort of ceremony but I never got it together. A Hindu friend did whatever Hindus do to help sick people. I used to feel caressed whenever someone would say "have a blessed day," which seems to be a favorite of African American women. Family and friends sent prayers by email and post and left prayers on my voice mail. People came to my hospital room and prayed. When I had my transplant, friends created prayers for me to say at this unique, truly once-in-a-lifetime life cycle event. For the last three to four years, I have been the most prayed-over non-celebrity in the universe. Each prayer mattered. Prayers have wings.

My own introduction to prayer began, naturally, in the midst of crisis. I had completed a round of chemo and my immune system had completely bottomed out. I contracted pneumonia and the doctors began blasting me with thermo-nuclear antibiotics. Basically, my future would be determined by whether the infection or my white blood cells would win what amounted to a three day race. A friend had given me a book of selected psalms that had been edited to make them particularly suited for people in crises, which is exactly where I was. I found the psalms and the accompanying text extremely comforting. I memorized the 23rd Psalm and would repeat it relentlessly. When I wasn't reading the psalms, I was holding the book. When I lay down on the bed, I placed the book on my chest as if it were an amulet. In my first prayer, if you can call it that, I pleaded with God to get me through this pneumonia. In return, I promised never again to eat shellfish or pork. He did and I haven't. I am convinced that he has been listening to my prayers ever since.

The Psalms became a major source of spiritual strength for me. I recite the 23rd Psalm aloud *basso profundo* every time I have a scan or a procedure. It sounds very eerie when it reverberates in a PET scan tube, especially the "though I walk through the valley of the shadow of death" part. I would also repeat four lines of a particular Jewish prayer ("Lord of the World," *Adon Olam* in Hebrew) as a kind of mantra. Even secular Jews recognize this prayer because it signals the end of the three and a half hour Sabbath service and constitutes the bugler's call to the buffet. The lines I would repeat are these:

To God's kind hand I pledge my soul
each time I sleep, again to wake,
and with my soul, this body here.
Adonai's love is mine, I shall not fear.

Those four lines could easily replace about 16 hours of prayer on Rosh Hashanah. They remind me that I am not alone in all this. That is all I want. Not to feel alone.

Getting My Aura Balanced

I MET A WOMAN at a Complementary Medicine conference who had a pouch hanging on a cord around her neck. I asked her what was in the pouch. She explained that the pouch held her guardian angels. Oh, I said, and wondered whether I had come to the right place. I now believe in angels, although I offer no opinion as to whether they can be carried in a small leather pouch around one's neck.

Cancer is its own world, and despite the concerted, determined, generous, and loving efforts of family and friends, the cancer patient is alone in it. I often imagined myself on a desert island with boatloads of my family and friends sailing by, waving and shouting encouragement. I had my whole world in my corner but I just couldn't shake feelings of profound isolation and loneliness. These feelings (and my adventurous wife) forced me to open myself to a range of experiences that would have been nothing but comedy material for me years before.

I don't know exactly how to describe my foray into "spirituality" except anecdotally. My introduction came via an audio tape by Deepak Chopra, a gift from a friend. In this tape, Chopra argues that just because something isn't scientifically provable, doesn't mean that it can't work.

Chopra acknowledges that "magic" might not work every time (that's why they call it magic and not science), but that doesn't mean it can't work some of the time, and if it works some of the time that's plenty good enough. He also makes a case for the existence of "another" world, a world of energy, existing apart from but in juxtaposition with the material world. In the early stages of my treatment I listened to this tape over and over again trying to get a better understanding of this other world. This other world of energy had to be better than the material world in which I was living as a sick man. I have not been dissuaded from this view just because Chopra now hawks a line of health food.

The notion of another universe of energy received reinforcement. In Houston I met a wonderful, brilliant, and deeply philosophical woman who came to be a close friend. She and her husband had recently lost a son to cancer. Notwithstanding her recent loss, she was determined to be my guide and show me the administrative and treatment ropes at M.D. Anderson Cancer Center where her son, too, had been treated.

Bravely, she visited me in the hospital while I was getting treatment, and later, during my "recovery" periods in my hotel. We spent afternoons in conversation. She too had a belief in an unseen world of energy that could be accessed. In a gentle and intelligent way and without beating me over the head with a two-by-four, she led me to accept the possibility of such a world. Because it came from her, I knew this was an idea I had to take seriously.

The idea of an invisible non-material universe of energy underlies much of the "New Age" philosophy. No matter how you cut it, this idea seems weird and hard to accept. People who profess such things usually find themselves standing alone at cocktail parties with others pointing at them. This idea is different from the more conventional religious concept of "in heaven" in one important respect — you can access this "energy universe" while alive and I have tried to do so.

I have had different kinds of treatment from a variety of healers, all of whom share a common view: the material world is not the only one that exists. As a corollary, there is the notion that each of us has a colored energy field surrounding our body (aura) as well as an internal energy (chi) that can be directed and harnessed towards health and healing. These views are decidedly not part of the western medical model but are the foundation of many alternative healing arts, including acupuncture. Recent surveys have shown that a large number of Americans are accessing these and other other-than-western treatment systems.

People who could see such things told me that my "aura" was badly out of balance and discolored. While this diagnosis did not have the same effect as if my transplant doctor told me that an X-ray showed problems, still, I didn't like the idea of having anything out of balance. So I embarked on an "alternative" treatment course to fix the problem. Chopra argues that the mental and emotional "intention" you bring to an activity can affect the outcome. As hard as it was, I decided to "intend" that my alternative treatments would help me.

This, it turns out, was that hardest part — to actually believe that non-medical New Age approaches could work. It was like trying to believe in magic or, even worse, faith healing. There is something to be said for both.

The movie *The Man in the Moon* is about the life of the late comedian Andy Kaufman. Kaufman died of cancer at the age of 36. The movie depicts Kaufman getting treatment from a guru-type who places colored crystals at strategic locations on his body. Kaufman asks for more blue. I remember thinking how desperate Kaufman must have been to subject himself to such an obviously bogus procedure. P.S.: I now wear an amethyst around my neck. Amethyst is my healing stone because it is in my healing color — violet. I know this because my color and sound therapist told me. I was referred to him by my sister-in-law who told me that "everyone" in New York is going to him. That was good enough for me. This therapist does "accutone" which he describes as a kind of acupuncture with sound. This entails the recipient (me) listening to him sing or chant different colors at different pitches for differing periods of time. Something like: Bluuuuuuuuuuuuue, Red-Red-Red-Red, Whiiiiiite. For those who are familiar with such things, his chanting sounds a little like the Shofar or ram's horn that is blown on the Jewish New Year. The first time he did this for me, I couldn't help laughing. For his services, I paid him $80. Before *you* laugh, please take note that I have been told that this man now provides this service to kids at Sloan-Kettering Cancer Center. M.D. Anderson is experimenting with providing soothing music to patients as they receive chemo.

A dear friend of 25 years believes that she can relay a divine and healing light that offers a kind of spiritual purification. She would come to see me rain or shine to relay this light. She traveled to New York several times on her own nickel to treat me in the hospital after my transplant. More than that, she generally stalked me to make sure that I received a continual and therapeutic dose of "light" which, she told me, had a cumulative affect, like chemo. I always enjoyed her company and we talked intimately about many things. I don't know about the efficacy of the light, but it didn't matter. One way or the other, our sessions *always* left me feeling better.

My wife, Suzanne, fixed me up with a Brazilian healer whose specialty was getting the seven layers of the aura — your energy field — in balance. This, in turn, depended on getting your seven *chakras* (don't ask) righted. I would lie on a massage table as he placed his hands gently on my body while South American Indian music played. He invoked angels on my behalf. Archangel Gabriel was my personal angel, but there were other worker-bee angels too. Angels form an integral part of the Hebrew bible storyline, but disappear in the Jewish literature after that. Jewish scholars didn't want angels to assume too great an importance and so they were de-emphasized. When I was in treatment, I imagined an angel hovering over me, wings extended protectively. It was a comforting image. There was a Christian aspect to his treatment: religious icons were in the room, and he ended each session promising me that I would be protected by the blue light of Mohamed and the white light of Jesus. When he said that, I would silently sing a verse mantra from the *Adon Olam* prayer. I was startled to see my rigidity the first time this happened but decided to let it go. As long as he didn't sprinkle water on my forehead, I was OK with it. He also placed crystals strategically on my body. I had become Andy Kaufman.

I also did t'ai chi, acupuncture, and Reiki meditation. I received Reiki treatment from my Santa Fe sister- and brother-in-law, several massage therapists, and my belly dancing interior decorator. My brother-in-law arranged a session for me with a woman in Santa Fe named Sujata who is a channeler — exactly the kind of person the Hebrew Bible prohibits Jews from consorting with. I was extremely uneasy with this, but it turned out that the experience was more like psychotherapy than fortune telling.

Sujata was, after all, from New York. She helped me understand what to do with the fear I would feel from time to time and gave me advice on how to help my kids in the midst of the situation. I think this advice came from her and not anyone on the "other side." In Hindu literature, Sujata was a woman who gave water to Buddha as he was on a journey. My Sujata's was from New York where her origins were Jewish, naturally.

Recently, I sent my palm prints to my cousin in Vegas who is a professional palm reader and spiritual advisor. She has a large and successful practice and, I am told, many people will not take a step without a reading from her. She reads palms at our family Seders, right after the hand washing. I can't get three kids of the extended family to say the four questions but she has 35 people lined up to have their palms read. In the early '80s my cousin read Suzanne's palm and predicted that she would have a third child, a boy. Suzanne did. She also predicted that Suzanne would some day be faced with an overwhelming family crisis. She read my palm too, and didn't like my lifeline although she fudged a bit.

I was open to a lot, but not everything. I never took any naturopathic or herbal remedies. None of my medical doctors could tell me how they would affect my medical treatment and all were suspicious and negative. I met one naturopathic physician who wanted to get me off medical treatment and on a special bland bean and grain diet which I regarded as worse. No. If I was gonna go, I wanted to go with steak firmly between my teeth.

As with everything else in America, complementary and alternative therapies are now big business. The National Institutes of Health reports that 36% of adults in the United States use some form of complementary or alternative medicine. There are national conferences, Presidential reports, and thousands of practitioners of hundreds of different services, including my favorite, colonics. All the leading cancer centers now provide yoga, t'ai chi, massage, and meditation. This would have been unheard of years ago but the cancer industry knows that this is what people crave — a more spiritual and introspective healing process. Cancer centers are no different than other competitive commercial enterprises — you have to give the customers what they want.

AN APPRECIATION: NED STUTMAN (1945 - 2005)

From: Headfirst Baseball
September 27, 2005 3:03 PM

Dear Gamers Family,

Last week, we lost a special friend of our program when Ned Stutman passed away at the age of 60 after a long battle with mantle cell lymphoma.

Ned leaves behind a wonderful family — his wife Suzanne, sons Gabe and Zak, and daughter Shira, her husband Russ, and Ned's grandchildren, Caleb and Ma'ayan — along with an amazing legacy at the Justice Department's Office of Special Investigations. He also leaves an indelible mark on the Gamers.

Ned became a part of the Gamers in our first year, during the fall of 2001, when his son Gabe joined close friends Jake Alter (his teammate) and Tal Alter (his head coach) on our then 14U Gamers. In the years since, despite continuous battles with the cancer he was fighting so valiantly, Ned was a positive force on our sidelines — from St. Albans to Herndon to Southern Maryland to Pennsylvania to South Carolina — whenever he was able. His presence was such an uplifting one to coaches, players, and fellow parents alike — and he routinely took pride in the accomplishments of not only his son (there were plenty) or his Gamers team, but also our entire program.

In early August, less than two months ago, Ned, though his health was deteriorating, joined our oldest Gamers teams in Myrtle Beach for our final tournament of the summer. I sat with Ned and Gabe's big brother Zak for a few minutes at lunch and told him how strongly our staff all felt about Gabe, the anchor of our 18U Gamers — his work ethic, his blazing intelligence on and off the field, his leadership, his competitive fire. What I did not tell Ned was how strongly we all felt about Ned — his resilience, his omnipresent smile, his unwavering sense of humor, his undying support of the Gamers and our philosophies and ideals, his class. Ned was in so many ways exactly what a Gamer parent — what any parent of a young athlete — should be. He loved our program. And we loved him.

Later that week in Myrtle, Ned watched Gabe provide some late-inning heroics with a walk-off single to secure a win for our 18U boys. After the game, Ned returned to the hospital and then back home to D.C. It would be the last Gamers game he would see.

Thanks to so many of you, whether teammates of Gabe, coaches, or Ned's fellow parents and fans, who came to the funeral or shiva evenings last week. The turnout, as it should have been for such a special man, was unbelievable.

As the days move along this fall, please keep Ned, Suzanne, Gabe, and their family in your thoughts and prayers. We will never forget Ned's impact on our Gamers program, not only for giving us Gabe, but also for giving so much of himself.

Ned, we will miss you dearly. Thank you for all you have done and will continue to do for all of us.

With Love,
Brendan, Tal, Justin, John, Ryan & The Gamers

FOR NED STUTMAN
1945 - 2005

*At the one year memorial service for Ned in which the tombstone was
placed on the gravesite, Eric Jacobson, Ned's nephew, who was living in
London at the time, wrote the following to be read at the service.*

ki al tzedek yashuv mishpat
To turn righteous into law is an inheritance

"EVERYONE IS UNIQUE," Ned told me one day after trying his no-caf,
double caf, de-caf routine at Starbucks. Peering out at strangers in the D.C.
Metro moments later, he continued: "Everyone's an individual, EJ, everybody
is one of a kind." One never really knows what to expect from such comments,
but the replies didn't shake him. I can still hear his "ok, ok" or "I can work
with that." In the later years, he seemed acutely aware of the complexity and
originality of every human being, and he was somehow able to manifest this
in the most routine of everyday experience.

Even in Ned's grueling journey through the medical industry,
technicians, nurses, and physicians were being tended to as they were
tending. This was possible to see like the very top of his thoughts. Down
below lay a long series of observations, notes, and recognitions. The longer
he knew you, the greater his collection. He would give you a name and this
would be a special and unique name. The name meant that his collection
had reached a certain point. He would begin with something like "ok, EJ,
I'll tell you what we are going to do" and often it was something intimately
connected to what you mentioned to him. If it was something troubling
you, that "I'll tell you what we are going to do" was his way to free a weight
from your shoulders.

When I arrived at the Stutmans' in 2003, many of the treatments and trials were over. I was low too. My first real university position had set me on a downward spiral. My immediate boss was the tormented son of an English vicar who had made a small career by the selling of the legacy of the Holocaust for a handsome price. The opportunity to get away from that, in addtion to the chance to be with the Stutmans for what would be Ned's last years was a small miracle. Ned and I were on unproven ground since the time I decided to move to Berlin in 1993, but his sickness, as it sometimes does, managed to patch things up. By the time I made it to Washington that summer, Berlin seemed long ago. I was then not a survivor of the Blitzkrieg but of Brighton, and any mention of the place would sink my spirits. Once, as my boss's name was invoked, Ned saw his opportunity. Suddenly, with a booming voice, he announced: "Dr. Titties, did someone say Dr. Titties? I thought that's what someone said, Dr. Titties " and with that, all the pain and suffering was washed away in a moment, drowning out the name as one does with the villain of a Purim spiel.

Everything was in a name, and I think Ned began to realize this in his later years. This must have also impressed Francis X. Cluney of the *New York Times* when he asked Ned about Demjanjuk's claim of mistaken identity. The reply, which Cluney reproduced in the *Times*, was that of the Nazi hunter and chief prosecuting lawyer of Ivan the Terrible: "What identity thief would steal his own name?" I never got to ask Ned if he knew that both Demjanjuk and a doppelgänger impersonating the author made its way into Philip Roth's novel *Operation Shylock*. When I finally made it to the Stutmans, this also seemed like ancient past.

Ned gave his life for the pursuit of justice. He was convinced that his place on earth, his role in the preservation and fulfillment of God's creation, was the pursuit of justice in the Here and Now. This is what the idea of divine justice must mean. Whether in the protection of the disadvantaged or the prosecution of the wicked, Ned understood the pursuit of worldly justice as his purpose.

As the years progressed, I think Ned also understood this as a deeper and more profound manifestation of his faith in Judaism. The Talmud instructs the support of the orphan, the widow, and the stranger. Ned's task was to extend this principle to less recognized disabilities. In the prosecution of the crimes of the Nazis, Ned did what he could to keep God's promise *ki al tzedek yashuv mishpat* as expressed in Psalms 94:

> *For the Lord will not cast off his people, neither will he forsake his inheritance. But judgment shall return unto righteousness and all the upright in heart shall follow it. (Psalms 94.14-15)*

The essential part — *ki al tzedek yashuv mishpat,* to turn righteous into law — is an inheritance, and at the same time, a longing which represents his life work in kindness, in love and in the fulfillment of justice. It is an inheritance which, through his work, many of us share — those who knew him by name and those that will never know him — the unknown and unnamed of the past and the future generations who may benefit from his work in civil rights.

Woody Allen once said that his parents believed in two things: God and Wall-to-Wall Carpeting, and not necessarily in that order.

In Ned's case, I think it was Divine Justice and Chicken Parmesan, and probably in that order.

Eric Jacobson
10 July 2006

Engraved on the tombstone:

ישראל בן שמואל ובתיה

Adoring Husband, Father, Grandfather, Brother and Friend
Edward Alan "Ned" Stutman
April 6, 1945–September 17, 2005
His Humor and Compassion
Continue to Brighten Our
Memories and Instruct Our Lives

AFTERWORD

NED STUTMAN DIED on September 17, 2005.

There was no last-minute wonder drug, no against-the-odds recovery, just the lymphoma's tragic, inevitable conclusion.

The end of Ned's life didn't feel like the end — at least, not until the very end. "I lived in extreme denial and so did he," Suzanne Stutman, his wife, said. In the spring of 2005, she threw him a birthday party. As the cherry blossoms bloomed outside, friends and family gathered from all over the country in a Washington hotel ballroom to share their favorite Ned stories. "It was just totally a celebration of life," Shira Stutman, Ned's oldest child, said.

It wasn't until later that Ned's family understood how sick he had been at the time. Now, "What's most striking in terms of my dad's death is when we look back at pictures from four or five months before his death, is how sick he really looked," Shira continued. The doctors basically knew what was going to happen and when, but they kept it to themselves, letting the family carry on with as much normality as possible. "We knew he was going to die but it didn't hit us in any palpable way," Shira said.

Ned was mostly at home for the spring and summer, save for short hospital stays. He worked on this book, put his papers in order ("Maybe he knew the end was coming more than we did," Shira said), slept with Suzanne in the same bed they always had. His grandchildren, Caleb and Ma'ayan, were four and one years old at the time, and Ned held, read to, and took naps with them. He and Caleb threw balls around.

The Stutman and Shaw men

In June, Suzanne and Shira's family — Russell Shaw, her husband, and Caleb and Ma'ayan — went to Israel. Ned took a trip to North Carolina with his sons, Zak and Gabe, to watch Gabe play baseball with his longtime Washington team. At night, Ned would go to a local hospital to get enough blood to last through the following day. "People told me they were surprised that he went," Gabe said. "I wasn't really surprised at all. I would have been surprised that he didn't come. The strength of his personality would make you forget that his body was deteriorating."

It wasn't until days before Ned's death that the family understood what was approaching. "I got a call on Wednesday that the end was near," Shira said. "It was a shock. He died that Saturday morning."

The only person who seemed prepared was Ned. As soon as Russ walked into his hospital room that week, Ned told him to "get a pen and paper and sit down," Russ said. Ned fired off instructions: what his obituary should say (the headline could be "Justice Department Lawyer, Humorist"), who should write it, who should speak and sing at the funeral, who the pallbearers should be.

For a dying man, Ned was quite a flirt. He teased the nurses, a young female resident or two, and the two dozen or so close friends who filed in to say goodbye. When Rep. Henry Waxman came by, Ned asked for a kiss. ("I'm not afraid of your germs," he said.) Sometimes he would stop joking and start hallucinating. Then he would start joking again. "Tragedy and hilarity often bled together with my dad," Gabe said.

And Ned had important things to say to those he loved most. "Like with everyone, Ned managed to give me the sense that I was the one he wanted to see, that my visit was the one he had been waiting for," Russ said. "He could do that. Make you feel like you were *it* for him, and he was someone you wanted to be *it* for."

"In terms of saying goodbye, there was a strong sense, at least in me, of continuation," Gabe said. Though it was awful to witness the end of his father's life, "he left me with a lot to work with," Gabe said. "I just sort of had this feeling that yeah, his life ended and his body ended but I just felt responsibility and pride in what he's left me and in what I consider to be my responsibility to him and to the family. And it's not an obligation but a source of pride and passion."

Suzanne said she has only seen Gabe cry a few times in his life, and this was one of them. "Ned said, 'I love it that you're crying because I see that you love me, and this is the most important gift you could give to me.'"

The final moments were brutal. "Before my father was about to die, he was in a coma or something to that effect," Zak said. "He was drowning because his lungs were filling up with water. He was lying there in the hospital bed, the frailest he had ever looked, with one of those cheap bar mitzvah kippahs making his head look pointy. He was gasping for air. His eyes were closed. I crawled onto the bed and curled up next to him. I remember wanting the gasping to stop. I was scared by how sad I felt. Now, I wish I could hear him gasp again."

NED LEFT THE WORLD on a Saturday afternoon at 12 o'clock. Less than 48 hours later, hundreds of mourners filled the main sanctuary at Adas Israel Congregation in Washington. Instead of delivering a standard funeral oration, Rabbi Avis Miller had written what was essentially her own biography of Ned, taking the congregation from high school to his years of practicing civil rights law in Philadelphia to his prosecution of Nazi war criminals for the U.S. Department of Justice. The congregation looked heartbroken — except for during a few stories, like the time Ned had presented Suzanne with an engagement ring embedded in a bowl of tuna salad. Then they howled like audience members at one of Ned's comedy appearances.

When Shira, Zak, Gabe, and Russ rose to speak, they did not dwell on their own grief. Instead they asked their own friends to stand — the high school students and twentysomethings and thirtysomethings who had come to pay tribute to Ned. Dozens and dozens did.

"The beauty in his death is that everything was said that needed to be said," Suzanne said. Two years later, "I don't look back and say I wish we had done X."

As the family sat shiva, the notes and emails began to pour in. From former colleagues. Neighbors. Parents whose kids had shared classrooms with Ned's. Doctors, nurses. Everyone, it turns out, was convinced that they had a special relationship with Ned, that they were the one who shared an intimate bond or understanding with him. And then there were the people who did not know Ned but had heard about him and wanted to mark his passing.

There were too many letters to include here. They fill several binders. But they go something like this:

Paul Taskier wrote to remember the time he ran into Ned at the market on Friday afternoon. The store had run out of challah, so Ned gave him one of the family's two loaves so that his Sabbath table would not be without.

Writing at 3:30 in the morning, Kyla wrote about the first time she had heard of Ned Stutman, "this Nazi hunter who was the funniest lawyer in D.C. ... I figured, here is a guy who sounds like he had the perfect job for a Jewish lawyer — and he is undoubtedly funnier than I am. Like any good Washingtonian, I thought, 'How am I going to be able to compete with this guy?'"

Heather Kirkpatrick remembered the way he blessed his children at Sabbath dinner, placing his hands over their heads. "With those few moves he rose to the ranks of greatest father and husband in the world. He sits on that throne still."

Sveltana Schevchenko, an interpreter who had worked with Ned on war crimes cases, told of how she and Ned once got stuck at an iced-over airport deep in the Ukraine. Ned somehow befriended the governor of the local region and ended up throwing back shots of cognac with him — at seven o'clock in the morning.

IT'S BEEN OVER TWO YEARS NOW since Ned's death, his funeral, the shiva, the notes. Suzanne spent months reciting the Jewish prayers for the dead at a synagogue not her own, one where she wouldn't run into couples she knew or feel obligated to make small talk. She added more patients to her therapy practice, spent time with her grandchildren, and started doing all the things she had not done during Ned's long illness. Shira graduated from Rabbinical school. Zak became a doctor — another psychologist in the family — and Gabe started at Haverford College.

Nati shares her grandfather's birthday.

In the summer of 2006, Shira discovered she was unexpectedly pregnant. The baby was born on her grandfather's birthday: April 6. Her name is Natalia.

"He was ready to come back," Suzanne said.

For Jews, the Stutmans talk a lot about reincarnation. "My dad always said he was going to come back as a red bird," Shira said. The spring after he died, a cardinal made its nest right outside the family's window in Philadelphia, with babies soon following. Every time Caleb or Ma'ayan saw one, they would point to what they called the pop-pop birds.

The family is still grieving hard. At the burial, one of Zak's friends told him things would get easier with time. "In my mind, it seemed like that had to be true," Zak said. "Sometimes I think he was right. In other moments, I know he missed the point. Death is not linear. It sort of swirls, sucks you in, and then propels you in various directions. This seems to happen over and over and can be rather disorienting."

"We are still so sad," Shira agrees. "Especially when we have happy occasions. Things are almost perfect. But they will never, ever be perfect again." When the Stutmans eat together, Shira said, there are silences, the kinds of silences there never were before.

BUT THE FAMILY IS RECONSTITUTING itself, figuring out how to function without Ned, and nothing is static, not even his legacy. "The first year after his death, it was hard for me to remember him without thinking of his sickness," Gabe said. "But more recently, sometimes I'll just be doing something pretty random, I'll think of a joke that he would make in that situation and I'll start cracking up to myself."

For Russ, it's a question of trying on the habits of Ned's he loved most, figuring out how to make them his own. "There are times at the Shabbat dinner table, when we have lots of guests, that I try to channel Ned — the way he would look around the table, welcoming each person, making each feel like *she* was the reason this dinner was happening, that it was her presence that made it such a special night," Russ said. "When I do it, I know it's a weak imitation of the real thing, yet it still sanctifies moments in a way that I never would have been able to do without having had Ned in my life."

Even sitting on the couch with Ned, watching a football game no one particularly cared about, could somehow be vital and fun and memorable, Russ said. "He had a way of making you feel like you were at the best party in town."

Jodi Kantor
November 2007

APPENDIX

NED'S CAREER IN OSI

Remarks by OSI Director Eli Rosenbaum
at the funeral service for Ned Stutman, September 19, 2005

I'M VERY GRATEFUL FOR THE INVITATION that was kindly extended to me by Ned's family to tell you about his remarkable work at the Justice Department's Office of Special Investigations, pursuing justice on behalf of the victims of Nazi inhumanity. On the other hand, the task before me is a daunting one. Trying even to summarize Ned's amazing career at OSI in just a few minutes is a complete impossibility, so I will try instead to convey the *flavor* of it — or, to use a word that was one of his favorites: the *gestalt* of it. Whenever Ned used that German word at OSI — and he used it a lot — one got the sense that the irony was very much intended.

One way to describe Ned's decade-long tenure at OSI would be to recite some simple statistics and facts. A nutshell presentation of that sort would go something like this: Ned joined OSI in 1992, after distinguished careers as an attorney in the Justice Department's Civil Rights Division and, before that, at Health, Education and Welfare and in various state and local government positions in Pennsylvania, including a stint as an Assistant District Attorney in Philadelphia, working with renowned prosecutors like Arlen Specter and

Ed Rendell. As a Senior Trial Attorney at OSI, Ned investigated dozens of cases of suspected Nazi criminals and he took the lead in developing and/ or litigating 13 citizenship revocation prosecutions all around the country against World War II-era Nazi perpetrators, *all* of which ended in victories for the Government. That's right: we won *every single one* of those exceedingly complex cases. Most notably, he spearheaded the development of a series of enormously important cases concerning the notorious Nazi facility at Trawniki, Poland — literally, a school for mass murder, at which the SS trained men to implement Hitler's genocidal "Final Solution" against Jews in Poland. Ned played a key role in devising the legal arguments and litigation strategies that have led to success in those cases, based largely on captured Nazi records and other documents uncovered after the fall of the Iron Curtain.

Describing a pair of Ned's more famous cases will perhaps give you a better idea of his stellar accomplishments. He was the lead prosecutor in OSI's citizenship revocation case against Jacob Reimer, which went to trial in Manhattan in 1998. Reimer had served as a non-commissioned officer at Trawniki and had taken part in the liquidation of the Warsaw and Czestochowa Jewish ghettos. By his own admission in a sworn and tape-recorded pre-trial confession, this thrice-promoted SS auxiliary had also led a platoon of his own men on a mission to, as Reimer himself put it, "exterminate a Jewish labor camp." Ned's team successfully traced one of Reimer's men, Nikolai Leont'ev, to a small town deep in the frozen steppe of Russia, 12 hours by train from Moscow. On January 5, 1998, in dead of winter, and risking their lives to venture through an area then frequented by armed bandits, Ned and his OSI colleague Dr. David Rich travelled to Penza, Russia, to interview Leont'ev — himself a mass murderer. Leont'ev told his OSI interviewers about how Reimer was one of the leaders at a gruesome mass shooting of Jewish men, women and children, carried out in a wooded area near Lublin, Poland.

UNFORTUNATELY, HOWEVER, by the time the case went to trial, Reimer brazenly recanted his confession. To make matters worse, the judge refused to allow Reimer's tape-recorded confession into evidence, and he chose to give no weight at all to Leont'ev's testimony. The fate of one of OSI's most important prosecutions now rested almost entirely on Ned Stutman's shoulders. Specifically, the only hope for the Government to prevent the defendant's getting away with his horrible crimes lay in the remote possibility of shaking Reimer's carefully rehearsed testimony in the courtroom. After Reimer's own attorney finished taking him methodically through the Q&As that they had choreographed with impressive precision, the prospects looked grim indeed for the Government. Of course, the outcome of the story is by now obvious: Ned's relentless questioning, powered by his complete mastery of the case record, left Jacob Reimer hopelessly tangled up in his web of mutually contradictory tales and he at last acknowledged, in open court, that he had, after all, taken part in a mass shooting. We won the case. Thus did history catch up with Jacob Reimer, some 60 years after he had ensured that none of his victims would live to tell of his crimes.

Ned also served as lead counsel in the re-prosecution of former Nazi death camp guard John Demjanjuk. *The Washington Post* termed the 1999 refiling of this highest-profile of all OSI cases "courageous." Ned was our obvious choice to lead the prosecution. He was meticulous in his preparation, he already had considerable expertise in the underlying facts of the case, and we knew that not even Michael Tigar, Demjanjuk's famously talented and aggressive defense attorney, could undermine Ned's composure in court. On the first day of trial in Cleveland four years ago, Ned delivered a stirring opening statement inside a packed federal courtroom. Not until that afternoon, however, did he tell his trial team what he had learned just *before* he'd gone to court that very morning — namely, that the mysterious ailment that had dogged him for months was a very dangerous form of cancer. Who among us would have, or could have, done what Ned did — stayed at trial to outline the Government's case to the court — within an hour or so of learning that his life was in grave danger. This case too was won by the Government, based primarily on the superb work that Ned, co-counsel Jonathan Drimmer, and their team did to develop the case, prepare it for trial, and try it. Just a few months ago, Demjanjuk was ordered deported. Demjanjuk's case is but one of many in which we will carry on the noble quest for justice and fairness that was at the heart of every single job in which Ned Stutman was employed in the more than three decades since he graduated from law school in 1971.

Ned won a raft of Criminal Division special achievement awards while at OSI, and in 1997 he received the Assistant Attorney General's Award for Special Initiative, for the splendid work he did to help lead the Justice

Department team in the Government's inter-agency effort, directed by then Treasury Deputy Secretary Stuart Eizenstat, to trace the fate of valuables looted by the Nazis, including gold ripped from the mouths of Holocaust victims in the Nazi camps. The OSI team that Ned helped lead made virtually all of the key investigative discoveries in that historic effort. Ned also was a founding member of OSI's discovery committee — as near to a thankless job as exists at the Justice Department, but one that is absolutely essential in ensuring that our prosecutions live up the highest ethical standards. Ned always led by example in ethical matters and that's why Susan Siegal and I also chose him to be OSI's ethics officer, a position he filled with great distinction. Ned was truly as devoted to guaranteeing that our defendants got a fair shake from their prosecutors as he was to actually prosecuting those same defendants. I can think of no higher praise that can be given to a prosecutor. Ned brought honor to himself and to all of us at the Department of Justice.

THOSE, THEN, ARE THE BARE FACTS of Ned Stutman's extraordinary career at OSI. Alas, however, not only does a summary like the one I have just presented fail to mention many, many thousands of things that Ned did, so very effectively, in pursuit of justice while at OSI, it also conveys nothing of the very long hours he worked; of the ghastly accounts of Nazi horror that he was forced to confront on almost a daily basis; of the ingenuity, tenacity and great professional poise that he brought to his work; of Ned's uncanny ability to remain calm even when his colleagues — myself included — were in a panic. It doesn't tell you how Ned remembered the names of his colleagues' spouses and children, and inquired about them all the time. It doesn't tell you how Ned could bring a staff meeting to a complete and protracted halt with a single brilliant and thoroughly hilarious interjection. Or how our interns always gravitated to Ned, both to learn from him and to be entertained, as this man who was once voted Washington's Funniest Lawyer "held court" almost every summer day during lunchtime in OSI's conference room. (In Ned's characteristically modest way, he tried to minimize this comedic achievement by telling us that the less than uproariously funny Ed Meese had come in second, but we never believed him.) Worst of all, it tells you nothing of the deep and abiding sense of humanity that Ned demonstrated both in the causes to which he devoted his life and in his relationships with his colleagues. As so many others have said, he was, without doubt, what might be called the "spiritual heart and soul" of OSI. He was also surely the single most beloved person who ever worked at OSI. I know of not a single colleague with whom Ned worked (I'm not sure I even know of any opposing counsel) who did not love this man, whose gentleness and countless acts of kindness were surely his hallmark. Our Holocaust survivor witnesses loved him. Our interns loved him. We all loved him.

Ned taught us innumerable professional lessons and he taught us about what's important in life: earning the love of family and friends. He showed us so much love, and oh how we loved him back and how we miss him now. Finally, he taught us about courage.

Those of us who have been privileged to call Ned Stutman colleague and friend know that he will live on always in our hearts. To Suzanne, Zack, Shira, Gabe, and the entire family of which Ned was so obviously and so rightfully proud, all of us at OSI send our deepest condolences and our affection. And to Ned, we say: Thank you — for everything. And oh yes, as I and many others got to say to him many times over the years: *Love you, man.*

ACRONYMS
& GLOSSARY

Adon Olam (Hebrew), "Master of the World." First two words of a concluding hymn, presenting in poetic form the relationship between God, the world, and man. It was Ned's favorite prayer.

Ahl Cheyt (Hebrew). First words of a formulaic statement of sins committed during the previous year, spoken by the entire community on Yom Kippur.

Bar Mitzvah A boy at age 13 who is responsible for observing the commandments of Judaism. **Bat Mitzvah** A girl at age 12 who is responsible for observing the commandments required of a woman. These terms are also used to refer to the ceremony in the synagogue marking this rite of passage for the boy or girl.

Bimah (Hebrew), "platform." Synagogue dais holding the reading table for the Torah, where much of a religious service is conducted.

Book of Life Where God is said to inscribe the names of the righteous. Jewish tradition teaches that God writes the names of those who will live through the coming year in the Book of Life during the days between Rosh Hashanah and Yom Kippur. How one acts during these "Ten Days of Repentance" may influence God's decree. Referred to in Psalms 69:29.

Brit Milah (Bris–Hebrew). Ritual of circumcision of a baby boy on his eighth day, the day he enters into the covenant between God and Israel.

Caneel Bay Rockefeller-founded resort on the island of St. John in the Caribbean.

Challah (Hebrew). Egg-based braided bread. Two loaves are placed on the Shabbat dinner table and a blessing is recited over them.

Chasid (pl. **Chassidim**) Particular Orthodox Jew. Recognizable by the black coats and hats worn by most men. "Chasid" derives from the Hebrew word for loving kindness. Chassidim emphasize the joy of performing the commandments.

Chavurah (pl. chavuroth) (Hebrew), "fellowship." Small, informal group of Jews who assemble for Shabbat and holiday prayer services, communal experiences such as lifecycle events, and Jewish learning. Chavuroth provide an alternative to established synagogues and Jewish denominations. Most chavuroth emphasize egalitarianism, participation by the entire community, often without a Rabbi.

Conservative Judaism One of four main branches of Judaism in the U.S.: Orthodox, Conservative, Reform and Reconstructionist. Conservative Judaism positions itself between the more and less traditional branches.

DOJ - Department of Justice

Gabbai (Hebrew). Assistant in the running of a synagogue, particularly the Torah service.

Hemogloblin (HGB) Protein in red blood cells responsible for transporting oxygen through the body.

Hillel and Shammai Two of the most revered Rabbis of their time (the beginning of the first century C.E.). They studied together in Palestine and wrote many significant treatises, often disagreeing, on the law and on life.

Hol Ha-Moed The intermediate days of Passover and Sukkoth. The restrictions of the first and last days, which are similar to Shabbat, do not apply.

Hondle (Yiddish), "to bargain." As in "If you hondle long enough, you'll get a lower price."

Kosher (Hebrew), "fit," or "in proper condition." A designation for food permitted to be eaten in accordance with Jewish dietary laws.

Maccabees Jewish rebels in Jerusalem who led a successful revolt in 164 B.C.E. against the anti-Semitic oppression of the Syrian King Antiochus. Hanukkah commemorates the rededication of their Temple when a small cruse of oil, sufficient enough for only one day, burned for eight days.

Macrobiotic Simple, balanced diet that professes to offer health and longevity. Followers of the macrobiotic lifestyle try to observe balance in everything they do, living in harmony with people, nature and their physical surroundings.

Mazal Tov (Hebrew), "good luck." Congratulatory expression offered on happy occasions and good news.

Mi Sheberiakh Blessing for sick people. Recited during the reading of the Torah, asking God for the speedy recovery of an ill person.

Michio Kushi Born 1926 in Japan, he helped bring modern macrobiotics to the U.S.

Omer Ancient Hebrew unit of dry measure for crops, about 3.5 liters. It gives its name to the period of 49 days, from the second night of Passover until the night before Shavuot, when newly-harvested barley is offered in the Temple on behalf of the Jewish people. This is known as "counting the Omer."

OSI - Office of Special Investigations Since 1979, a branch of the Criminal Division of the U.S. Department of Justice. Its purpose is to detect and investigate individuals who took part in Nazi-sponsored acts of persecution before and during World War II, and who subsequently entered, or seek to enter, the U.S. illegally and/or fraudulently. OSI takes appropriate legal action to exclude, denaturalize and/ or deport perpetrators.

Platelets Blood components that play an important role in clotting. Patients with insufficient platelets have an increased risk of excessive bleeding and bruising.

RBCs - Red Blood Cells Donut-shaped cells that contain hemoglobin. Insufficient RBCs cause anemia, fatigue and weakness. Extreme cases of too many RBCs can interfere with the flow of blood.

Reiki A form of healing touch. Reiki is a style of spiritual practice, often compared to faith healing, proposed for the treatment of physical, emotional and mental diseases.

Rosh Hashanah "The Head of the Year," the Jewish New Year. Rosh Hashanah marks the beginning of the Ten Days of Repentance, culminating with Yom Kippur. During these ten days, God remembers all His creatures and passes judgment on all human beings, thus determining their lot for the year to come. These two holidays are commonly referred to as the High Holidays.

Schlep (Yiddish), "to carry." **Chrome schlepper** Ned's word for the pole that holds a cancer patient's bag of intravenous chemotherapy medicine.

Seder (Hebrew), "order." Ceremony held in Jewish homes on the first two nights of Passover (one night in Israel). The centerpiece of the Seder is the reading of the Haggadah, the retelling of the Exodus of the Jews from Egypt.

Shabbat (Hebrew), "Sabbath." The seventh day of the week when Jews are commanded to cease work just as God ceased his work of Creation on the seventh day. It is a foundation of Judaism. Shabbat, a day of physical and spiritual joy, begins at sundown Friday and ends at sundown Saturday.

Shavuot (Hebrew), "weeks." Spring holiday that falls exactly 50 days after Passover. It commemorates the giving of the Ten Commandments (and more) to the newly-freed Hebrew slaves at Mt. Sinai. As a prelude, Jews are commanded to "count the Omer" (see **Omer**).

Stem Cells Immature blood cells common to all multi-cellular organisms that retain the ability to renew themselves through cell division and can differentiate into a wide range of specialized cell types.

Sturm and Drang (from German), commonly translated as "Storm and Stress." German literature and music movement taking place from the late 1760s through the early 1780s.

T'ai Chi A Chinese martial art form.

Tefillin (Hebrew). Also called by the Greek **phylacteries**. Two black leather cubes, containing text from the Torah, with long leather straps that are wrapped in place on the forehead and left arm during the daily morning prayer (except for Sabbath and holidays) by Jewish males, and some females, over the age of thirteen. Wearing the Tefillin conforms with a Biblical commandment (Deuteronomy 6:4) and is a reminder that the Torah must be studied and obeyed every day.

Torah Also called **Pentateuch**, or Five Books of Moses. The first five books of the Bible. Torah reading is the centerpiece of the Shabbat morning service. Each year the Torah is read aloud in its entirety in synagogue.

WBC - White Blood Count Amount of white blood cells in total blood volume; about 1% of the blood in a healthy adult.

WBCs - White Blood Cells Also **leukocytes**. Immune system cells that fight infection and injury. Over- or underproduction of WBCs can cause blood diseases. Leukemia and mantle cell lymphoma are caused by too many WBCs.

Yom Kippur The holiest day of the Jewish year. A fast day when Jews ask for forgiveness.

CANCER CENTERS

Fred Hutchinson Cancer Research Center (the "Hutch")
University of Washington, Seattle, Washington
www.fhcrc.org

Johns Hopkins Hospital
Baltimore, Maryland
www.hopkinshospital.org

Lombardi Cancer Center at Georgetown University
Georgetown University Medical Center, Washington, D.C.
http://lombardi.georgetown.edu

M.D. Anderson Cancer Center (MDA or MDACC)
Houston, Texas
www.mdanderson.org

Memorial Sloan-Kettering Cancer Center (S-K)
New York, N.Y.
www.mskcc.org